THE ARGYLL AND SUTHERLAND HIGHLANDERS

THE
ARGYLL AND SUTHERLAND
HIGHLANDERS

A Concise History

TREVOR ROYLE

MAINSTREAM
PUBLISHING

EDINBURGH AND LONDON

First published in Great Britain in 2008 by
MAINSTREAM PUBLISHING COMPANY
(EDINBURGH) LTD
7 Albany Street
Edinburgh EH1 3UG

ISBN 9781845960902

A catalogue record for this book is available
from the British Library

Typeset in Bembo

Printed in Great Britain by
Clays Ltd, St Ives plc

Contents

Preface

In 2006 The Royal Regiment of Scotland came into being as a result of one of the many organisational reforms which have been visited on the British Army since its beginnings in the seventeenth century. Inevitably, those latest changes created a great deal of sadness in the army community and more widely throughout Scotland, with regret being expressed for the loss of some cherished names and the conversion of single battalion regiments into a new formation. However, the history of the British Army shows that the story of its regiments has been one of constant development, with cutbacks, amalgamations and changes of name being part of a process of evolution stretching back over several centuries. In every case the development has not led to a diminution of the army's capabilities but has produced new regiments which are the equal of their predecessors. The formation of The Royal Regiment of Scotland came 125 years after the last all-embracing reorganisation of the infantry under Edward Cardwell and Hugh Childers in 1881, when single battalion regiments were amalgamated and territorial names replaced the earlier system of numbering. As a result of those reforms – thought revolutionary at the time – The Argyll and Sutherland Highlanders (Princess Louise's) came into being by merging the 91st (Argyllshire) Highlanders with the 93rd (Sutherland) Highlanders under a common cap badge.

Together with the other books in the series, this concise history has been written to mark this latest transformation in Scottish and British military history. This is not a new regimental history of the regiment and its predecessors, but I hope it will be a useful addition to the regiment's historiography. Invariably, as is the case with the other concise regimental histories in the series, it also reflects the history of the British Army and the empire in which it served. I owe a tremendous debt to previous regimental historians, whose books are listed in the bibliography. It goes without saying, I hope, that the history of the regiment could not have been attempted without a thorough reading of these volumes as well as the many personal accounts written by soldiers who served in The Argyll and Sutherland Highlanders.

For help with the selection of illustrations I would like to thank the staff at Home Headquarters, especially Joyce Steel and Rod Mackenzie. Grateful thanks are also due to Major-General Andrew Graham, who gave his blessing to the project during his period of office as Colonel of The Argyll and Sutherland Highlanders.

Trevor Royle

ONE

The War against Napoleon

The Argyll and Sutherland Highlanders is the youngest of Scotland's infantry regiments and its two component parts were amongst the last of the British line regiments to be formed at the end of the eighteenth century. Both the 91st (Argyllshire) Highlanders (originally numbered 98th) and the 93rd (Sutherland) Highlanders were formed as the consequence of a government decision to utilise the military virtues of the Highlanders in the wake of the failed Jacobite rebellion of 1745–46 and the need to expand the British Army in the war against Napoleonic France at the end of the century. In its final form, the regiment came into being as a result of the 1881 reforms which created two battalion infantry regiments through a process of amalgamation (see Chapter Four) and it is usually known simply as the 'Argylls'. Most of its recruits were drawn originally from the counties which give the regiment its name but it also enjoys a long association with Stirlingshire, the central belt and Glasgow, its final headquarters being at Stirling Castle. From those areas the regiment created its own character, a mixture of solid Highland values with the added ingredient of west of Scotland industrial toughness and hard-headed realism. Other factors contribute to its individuality: the six tassels on the sporran (known as the swinging six); the green silk ribbon on the kilts worn by officers and senior NCOs; the regimental mascot, a Shetland pony called Cruachan; and the badger-headed sporrans worn by officers and sergeants.

But it is deeds, not uniforms and traditions, which give a regiment its reputation. A high profile comes from the way soldiers behave and not from their appearance and on that score the Argylls have not disappointed their many admirers. Two incidents, more than many others, have helped to bring the regiment to prominence. The first occurred during the Crimean War of 1854–56, when Britain and France deployed expeditionary forces to support the Ottoman Empire during a period of threatened Russian expansion in the Balkans and the Black Sea region (see Chapter Three). Amongst the regiments serving in the Highland Brigade under the command of Brigadier-General Colin Campbell was the 93rd (Sutherland) Highlanders, and its moment in history came on 25 October 1854 during the Battle of Balaklava. The day had begun well, with a heavy bombardment of the Russian positions inside the port and fortress of Sevastopol, but it ended badly, with a dreadful blunder which led to the destruction of the British Light Cavalry Brigade.

But against that loss, which only contributed a small part to the fighting at Balaklava, there was the heroic resistance of the 93rd, which repulsed a determined attack on the British positions by the Russian's 6th Hussar Brigade under the command of Major-General Rijov. As the Russian cavalrymen formed up for the charge Campbell reminded his men that there was no escape and they would have to die where they stood. Demonstrating great courage and excellent marksmanship, the Highlanders drove off the Russian cavalry and in so doing earned themselves an immortal role in British military history. Their feat was witnessed by William Howard Russell, the war correspondent of *The Times*, and his report of the action described the Highlanders as 'that thin red streak topped with a line of steel'. Soon it entered the language as 'the thin red line' and was later used to describe any act of heroism in which British soldiers faced overwhelming odds.

The second high-profile incident came 113 years later, in the dying days of British colonial rule in South Arabia (see Chapter Ten). During the early 1960s Britain had established the Federation of South Arabia as a first step to prepare Aden and its protectorates for independence, but the area was soon embroiled in an increasingly bitter insurgency war. Matters came to a head in June 1967 when the police mutinied and the Crater district fell into the hands of armed dissidents. A number of British soldiers were killed in the incident but the position was restored when 1ˢᵗ Argyll and Sutherland Highlanders retook Crater under the command of Lieutenant-Colonel Colin Mitchell. Like the thin red line at Balaklava, the incident received widespread press coverage (more so given the advent of radio and television) and the regiment became headline news across the world, not least because Mitchell had a knack for securing publicity. Once again a high-profile action had made the Argylls one of the best-known regiments in the British Army.

However, what happened in the Crimea and Crater should not detract from countless other acts of courage and endurance which have punctuated the regiment's history since it came into being at the end of the eighteenth century. The move to recruit Highland soldiers into the British Army had begun during the Seven Years War (1756–63) when the prime minister, William Pitt the Elder, acting on a suggestion made by King George II, opened the door for the creation of the Highland regiments. Highlanders were regarded as good soldiers, their powers of endurance and fighting qualities had become evident during the earlier Jacobite rebellions. Here was an untapped and ready supply of soldiers who would do their duty while their clan loyalties would bring a sense of coherence and reliability which would translate into good military practice. As the days of the clan system were numbered after Culloden and would soon disappear, other than as a sentimental entity based on chiefdoms, tartan and yearning for a lost past, the Highland regiments became handy substitutes.

Not that their creation was universally popular, either in England or in Scotland. Memories of Highland violence and savagery were still vivid, but Pitt argued that the recruitment of the Highlanders served two purposes – a steady supply of good soldiers for service in Europe, North America and India and a means of finally pacifying a previously troublesome area by ridding it of its warlike young men. If they were killed in the process, then that might be no bad thing either: it was clear that many Highlanders would not return to their native lands, especially if they were fighting in colonial wars. Once the regiments were disbanded or returned to Britain many Highland soldiers settled in America, where it was hoped they would provide a loyal bulwark against any secession movement. Within the space of 20 years, once-rebellious and troublesome Highlanders found that they had been transmogrified into loyal patriots in the service of the Crown.

From the very outset of the process the territorial links of the regiments were vital, not just for recruiting but also for maintaining group cohesion and loyalty. The system had other benefits. Landowners who had supported the Jacobites were able to demonstrate their loyalty by raising regiments as a quid pro quo. Most considered themselves to be Highland gentlemen and if estates had been forfeited the raising of a regiment was a useful means of retrieving family honour and making good lost ground. That was an important consideration, as the creation of a regiment depended on social status and financial capacity, the going rate for raising and equipping a regiment being £15,000, an enormous sum which is worth nearly £1.5 million today. A landowner wishing to raise a regiment had to have contacts at the highest social level, as it was the king who gave authority for the regiment to be raised in his name. Once the order and warrant had been issued the regiment came into being and the commanding officer set about recruiting. For the senior officers a regimental commander would look to his closest family and friends and they in turn helped to recruit the soldiers from the tenants on their estates.

It worked, too. Between 1714 and 1763 a quarter of the officers serving in the British Army were Scots, proportionally more than the English. Of 208 officers who were also members of parliament from 1750 to 1794, 56 were Scots. At the same time, one in four regimental officers were Scots, and Scots were used to receiving high command while fighting in the European and colonial wars waged by Britain throughout the eighteenth century. Between 1725 and 1800 no fewer than 37 Highland regiments were raised to serve in the British Army and by the end of the period the numbers involved are estimated at 70,000 men. To put those figures into a local perspective, the records of the Adjutant-General in 1837 show that in the first four decades of the nineteenth century the Isle of Skye produced 21 lieutenant-generals and major-generals, 45 lieutenant-colonels and 600 majors, captains and subalterns in addition to 10,000 private soldiers.

91ST HIGHLANDERS

In 1793 Britain entered into 22 years of war against revolutionary France with a small, ill-equipped and demoralised army which had to take on an enemy whose armed forces numbered half a million. Years of cutbacks and inefficiency had left it with an army which Lord Macaulay described in his *History of England* as 'the laughing stock of all Europe' and in the opening rounds of the war against the French its reputation did not improve, with a series of disasters in Europe and some half-hearted exploits in the West Indies. Having cut back the size of the army in the wake of the earlier loss of the American colonies, steps had to be taken to raise new regiments and to add additional battalions to existing regiments. One of those regiments which came into being was raised by John Campbell, 5th Duke of Argyll, whose father had led the Campbell forces on the government side at the Battle of Culloden in 1746. Now in his 70s, the duke gave the task of raising the new formation to his kinsman, Duncan Campbell of Lochnell, a former Foot Guards' officer, who set about the not inconsiderable task of recruiting the necessary 1,064 men to form the new regiment. Each recruit had to be over five feet four inches in height and aged between 18 and 35. The task was made more difficult by the fact that another regiment, the 74th Highlanders (later 2nd Highland Light Infantry) had already been formed under the duke's sponsorship in 1787 and it proved to be difficult to get sufficient recruits from the traditional clan area. Additional recruits had to be found in Edinburgh and Glasgow, and when the regiment was formed in July 1794 only one third of its 741 soldiers came from the Highlands, while the majority of the officers were Scots (14 of their number were Campbells). Despite those problems, the regimental records show that there was a decent contribution of Highland names, with 50 Campbells, 26 McLeans, 25 MacDonalds, 22 McCallums, 16 McKenzies, 14 Robertsons and 12 McPhails.

The new regiment was numbered 98th and its first move was to the south of England to await orders for service overseas. In common with the other Highland regiments raised during the same period it wore belted plaids of the distinctive black and dark-green government tartan, red jackets with buff facings, red and white diced hose and a bonnet 'cocked and ornamented with ostrich feathers and with a diced border of red, white and green'. Officers were dressed in similar fashion and carried a basket-hilted broadsword. While the regiment was based at Chippenham in Wiltshire it added to its establishment from the local male population, thus beginning a tradition of turning non-Scots into proud wearers of the kilt. When the regiment was eventually fit for overseas service it numbered 32 officers, 35 sergeants, 22 drummers and 759 rank and file.

At that stage the war had not been going well for Britain. An expeditionary force of British and Hessian regiments commanded by the Duke of York, King George III's second son, had been despatched to Flanders to support the Austrian army fighting against the French but although they gave a good account of themselves under difficult circumstances they were outnumbered three to one by the French army under the command of General Jean Houchard. A series of exhausting marches and counter-marches dominated the campaign (which was memorialised in the children's nursery song 'The Grand Old Duke of York'), and following the surrender of Brussels and Antwerp to the French in July 1794 York's army was forced to withdraw to Britain. With the French holding the upper hand in the Netherlands, Dutch republicans threw in their lot with the French. The new strategic situation forced Britain to rethink its priorities and, unable to take the war back to Europe, the decision was taken to attack enemy assets in other parts of the globe.

As a result, the 98th was ordered to proceed to South Africa, where the resident Dutch colonists had sided with France and now posed a threat to British interests in the country. On 5 May 1795 the regiment left Spithead on board the East Indiamen *General Coote*, *Deptford* and *Warren Hastings* as part of the new expeditionary force under the command of Major-General Alured Clarke, and three months later the men had their first sight of South Africa when their ship made landfall at Simon's Bay to the south of Cape Town.

THE ARGYLL AND SUTHERLAND HIGHLANDERS

First impressions were auspicious. The regimental surgeon was reminded of his native hills of Moidart, adding the rejoinder that 'if possible the hills here are more barren; then there are very extensive plains, mostly sand, which are by no means inviting'. There was plenty of time to enjoy the view, as the regiment did not disembark immediately and was not in action until September, when it took part in fighting against the Dutch colonists at Wynberg. This short and sharp action was the beginning and the end of the operation as the opposition melted away and surrendered. Four men of the 98th were wounded during the action. Following the cessation of hostilities the regiment remained in South Africa for six years and during this period, in 1798, it was renumbered and renamed as the 91st (Argyllshire Highlanders). Being on active service in hot-weather operations, Highland dress was no longer worn and instead the men were dressed in the same red coats and white trousers as the rest of the British infantry.

In 1802 there was a temporary peace agreement with the French which was sealed by the Treaty of Amiens and under its terms the Dutch possessions in South Africa were returned. As a result, the 91st sailed back to Britain the following year although, as was the custom at the time, many of its men transferred to regiments bound for service in India. Being greatly depleted the regiment began recruiting but, like other regiments, it found that the supply of available men was finite. This was particularly true of Highland Scotland. In the period 1779–80, 13,586 men from north of the Highland Line had enlisted in their local regiments but this figure had dropped to 8,615 in the period 1803–04. This shortage forced the 91st to look elsewhere, to England and Ireland, to make up its numbers, and it was also helped by the transfer of men from the part-time militia and volunteer forces. In 1804 a 2nd battalion was raised, but this was used primarily to provide a flow of manpower into the 1st battalion.

THE WAR AGAINST NAPOLEON

By then war had broken out again with France, where Napoleon Bonaparte had become the undisputed leader. Having cowed most of Europe, his ultimate aim was to invade Britain with an army 200,000-strong which included his most experienced field commanders, including the future marshals Bernadotte, Soult and Ney. It was a moment of supreme danger, but in October 1805 the enterprise was foiled by Admiral Lord Nelson's famous victory at Trafalgar, where the French and Spanish fleets were destroyed. During the emergency the 91st served as part of the defences in southern England, an experience which most of the men found mind-numbingly dull. The 1st battalion was deployed briefly to northern Germany in December 1805 as part of an expeditionary force sent to aid Prussia but it was soon withdrawn without seeing any action. This was followed by an 18-month period of service in Ireland, where the companies were scattered across the country in small garrisons at Fermoy, Mallow, Cashel, Enniscorthy and Dublin. This period came to an abrupt end in the early summer of 1808, when the 91st found itself involved in the fighting in Spain and Portugal against Napoleon's battle-hardened veterans.

To complete Napoleon's plans for the total blockade of Britain, a plan known as the Continental System, it was essential that France should shut off the Iberian peninsula. After the renewal of hostilities in 1803 France had quickly defeated Prussia, Austria and Russia, and to complete the domination of Europe Napoleon turned his attention to Spain and Portugal. The first was subjugated by forcing the Spanish King Charles IV to abdicate and imposing military rule on the country under Napoleon's brother, Joseph. Portugal, England's oldest ally, was then invaded from Spain by an army commanded by Marshal Junot. Both were daring plans but both were foiled by the refusal of the people of Spain and Portugal to accept French domination and by the British decision to assist them in resisting the invasion by sending forces under the command of Lieutenant-General Sir Arthur Wellesley, an experienced veteran of the wars in India. The first part of the campaign ended in farce. Following their defeat at Vimiero on 21 August 1808, the French army was allowed to retreat back to France in ships provided by the Royal Navy. The agreement allowed Napoleon to assume command of military operations in the Peninsula. At the same time a new British force under the command of Major-General Sir John Moore marched from Lisbon into northern Spain through Salamanca towards Valladolid, his aim being to link up with friendly Spanish forces. In July 1808 the 91st sailed for Portugal, where it joined 5 Brigade under the command of Brigadier-General James Catlin Craufurd.

Almost immediately things started to go awry. Not only were the British forces ill-prepared to make a deep incursion into Spain but the French had not been idle. Napoleon had assembled a huge army of 250,000 men and in December he moved rapidly against Moore's smaller force of 20,000, taking with him 80,000 crack troops of the 'Old Guard' and two of his best marshals, Soult and Ney. The French moved fast and boldly towards the north-west and by the time Moore reached Salamanca he realised that he was badly outnumbered – reinforcements had been delayed and did not disembark until the beginning of November – and that Napoleon was now within striking distance. Initially, Moore hoped to attack a smaller French force under Soult at Burgos, but the move only stung Napoleon into a greater determination to crush the British. On Christmas Eve Moore received further intelligence of Napoleon's intentions: the French army had crossed the Guadarrama Mountains and were less then 20 miles away. If he continued he would risk annihilation, and so the order was given to fall back on Corunna, where the navy had been ordered to evacuate them.

So began an epic retreat across the snow-covered mountains.

THE WAR AGAINST NAPOLEON

It was an operation which demonstrated great courage and determination but it was also marred by scenes of drunken rampaging as the British soldiers looted the areas through which they passed. In a general order issued on 27 December, Moore told his men that he could 'feel no mercy towards officers who neglect, in times like these, essential duties, or towards soldiers who injure the country they are sent to protect', but the regimental records show that in this respect there was no need for the strictures to extend to the 91st, which was now under the overall command of Major-General the Hon. Edward Paget.

> For twelve days these hardy soldiers under Paget had covered the retreat, during which time they traversed eighty miles of road in two marches, passed several nights under arms in the snow of the mountains, were seven times engaged, and now took the outposts, having fewer men missing from the ranks, including those who had fallen in battle, than any division in the army; an admirable instance of the value of good discipline.

By the year's end Moore's army had passed through to the relative safety of Astorga, and when Napoleon arrived in the same place on New Year's Day he realised that there would be no pitched battle as his enemy had escaped. Instead of continuing the pursuit he left the rest of the operation in the hands of Ney and Soult and, having been warned of a plot against him, returned to Paris. Two weeks later Moore reached Corunna to find that the fleet had been delayed. There was now no option but to engage the French; during the hard-fought battle Moore was mortally wounded and was carried to a rear area by Guardsmen and men of the 42nd. Of the 30,000 British soldiers who marched into Corunna and engaged the French in battle, some 24,000 were eventually evacuated.

THE ARGYLL AND SUTHERLAND HIGHLANDERS

It had been a difficult experience for the 91st, and there was further demoralisation when it returned to Britain. Due to the problems of raising sufficient Scottish recruits, the regiment lost its Highland status and became the 91st Regiment of Foot, its uniform indistinguishable from other line regiments of the British Army. Five other Highland regiments suffered a similar fate but in the case of the 91st the figures are perhaps misleading, as the regimental records show that between 1800 and 1818, 970 Scots were recruited as against 171 Englishmen, 218 Irishmen and 22 foreigners, mostly Germans. During the same period the 2nd battalion recruited 599 Scots, 168 Englishmen, 142 Irishmen and 197 foreigners. There was only one compensation: as the tartan had already been issued for new kilts, the 91st had them made up into trews and adopted a flat, black bonnet ornamented with a single feather.

In that guise the regiment took part in a disastrous expedition to capture the island of Walcheren in Flanders in July 1809. Not only did the British expeditionary force fail in its objective to destroy the French fleet which lay at anchor in Flushing, but hundreds of soldiers fell victim to fever. By September, 4,000 had died (10 per cent of the total), and the force was evacuated. The casualties in the 91st were 60, most of whom died as a result of contracting fever, and in September, of the 636 effectives, 205 were in hospital. For the next three years the 91st was based in the south of England and did not see active service again until September 1812, when it was ordered to return to Spain to join the army commanded by Viscount Wellington, as Wellesley had become following his exertions against the French during the past three years. (In 1809 he had returned to command a small British force to liberate Portugal and Spain and had won a string of stunning victories including Busaco, Fuentes de Oñoro, Ciudad Rodrigo and Badajoz.)

When the regiment arrived in Spain Wellington was preparing for the final phases of his campaign of liberation. On arrival the

91st joined the 6th Division and was placed in the same brigade as 42nd Highlanders (later 1st Black Watch) and 79th Highlanders (later 1st Queen's Own Cameron Highlanders). In May 1813 Wellington opened his offensive, which he hoped would take his forces north-east from Portugal towards the Pyrenees and then on into France. At the first battle, Vitoria, fought on 21 June, the 91st was held in reserve but it was involved in the pursuit phase towards Pamplona and played a leading role at the Battle of Sorauren, fought on 28 July. Sensing that Soult was attempting to take advantage of his widely dispersed forces, Wellington ordered the 6th Division to reinforce the weakened 4th Division, which had withdrawn from Roncesvalles towards Pamplona.

Fortunately, the French commander, Marshal Soult, was innately cautious and delayed making any attack on the British lines, as by the time he opened the French account at midday a fresh British division had arrived. Even so, Wellington's forces were outnumbered two to one, but the ferocity and strength of the British fire-power was no match for the attacking French divisions, which failed to make any headway. Fighting continued until late afternoon, leaving the French with 4,000 casualties while those sustained by the British were 2,652 killed or wounded. The losses to the 91st were 12 killed and 101 wounded. The action continued on the following day with an assault on the French left, backed by artillery fire from a point known as Cole's Ridge. This allowed Wellington to counter-attack up the Arga Valley, and Soult's forces were soon in disarray. Once the fighting died down Wellington described the action as 'a close-run thing', but the battle had been well directed, not least because the soldiers had taken great heart at seeing their commander in the thick of the action.

Soult was now forced to go on the defensive and formed his line between Maya and the coast to the north where he believed that the estuary of the River Bidassoa was impassable. Unfortunately for him this was precisely where Wellington decided to make his attack. Taking advantage of local intelligence, which suggested that parts of the estuary could be crossed at low tide, Wellington decided to cross the Bidassoa and move his army quickly towards the frontier with France. While the Light Division occupied the centre the 1st and 5th Divisions crossed the estuary with the 2nd and 6th Divisions on the left, respectively at Maya and Roncesvalles. The next obstacle was the River Nivelle, Soult's new defensive position along a line which ran from St Jean-de-Luz to the Mondarrain Mountains east of Urdax. During the resultant battle on 10 November the 91st was on the right but the breakthrough came in the centre, where the French were known to be weak. This time Wellington enjoyed numerical superiority and he used it to good effect, with nine divisions attacking along a five-mile front. The only losses in the 91st were four men killed and six men wounded.

With foul winter weather hampering operations Soult was allowed to withdraw to his next line of defence along the River Nive, where the French drew up their lines south of Bayonne. For this attack the 91st was in the centre and crossed the river by pontoon bridges on 9 December. The battle was fought over extremely muddy terrain and lasted three days, mainly because the armies were evenly matched and Soult took the opportunity to counter-attack the British right, which became isolated during the frequently confused fighting. For Wellington it was a hard-won victory and he was quick to praise the fighting qualities of his soldiers, saying that the difference between him and Soult was that 'when he gets into difficulty, his troops don't get him out; mine always do'. The British and their Spanish and Portuguese allies were now in France and the end of the war was at last in sight. Only the winter weather prevented them from finishing the task. On 27 February 1814 the French rearguard was seen off at Orthes and the way was open to Toulouse, which fell in the second week of April.

This was followed by the news that Paris had fallen to the Allies and Louis XVIII had been restored to the throne of France. With the fighting in Europe at last over, the 91st moved to Ireland but returned to France nine months later, after Napoleon escaped from imprisonment on Elba and made one final attempt to retrieve his lost power. The result was the Waterloo campaign and Wellington's famous victory, but to the regiment's chagrin it was held in reserve during the battle and could not claim it as a battle honour.

With the end of the war against Napoleonic France the 2nd battalion was disbanded, but before the war ended it had its own chance to see active service. Together with 4th Royal Scots the battalion was part of a British brigade sent to Stralsund in Prussia, and from there it marched west to join a force besieging Antwerp. During the operations the 2nd battalion took part in the unsuccessful operations to attack the fortress of Bergen-Op-Zoom. Four of the battalion's companies succeeded in storming the outer defences only to be beaten back by superior numbers. It could have been worse. The Regimental Colour was almost captured when the ensign carrying the flag was cut down but it was saved by the courage and quick-thinking of Sergeant-Major Cahill, who was rewarded by being commissioned in the field, an unusual occurrence.

93RD HIGHLANDERS

The last of the Scottish Highland regiments was raised in 1799 as the 93rd (Highland) Regiment of Foot but its military antecedents were long and honourable. It was recruited almost exclusively from the northern county of Sutherland, where two powerful landowners, the Earl of Sutherland and Lord Reay, had been responsible earlier in the century for raising the Sutherland Fencibles, a force which was well known for the height of its men and their soldierly bearing. The historian Major-General Sir David Stewart of Garth described them as an 'excellent, orderly

regiment of well-behaved serviceable men, fit for any duty'
and the novelist Sir Walter Scott used his journal to call them a
'regiment of Sutherland giants'. (One of their number was Samuel
McDonald, a native of Lairg, who was seven feet four inches tall.
Throughout the army he was known as 'Big Sam'.) When the call
came to raise a regiment of infantry from the county many of the
Fencibles transferred to the new formation while the rest came
from the clan lands, with their colonel, Major-General William
Wemyss of Wemyss, doing the duty on behalf of the 16-year-old
Countess of Sutherland. A cousin of the family, Wemyss had also
commanded the Sutherland Fencibles, and as Brigadier Cavendish
recorded in his history of the regiment, he clearly knew his men
intimately.

> With a large snuff-box in his hand and an attendant with
> a bottle of whisky [Wemyss] went along the ranks, and
> to every man whom he wished to enter the corps, he
> ordered snuff – the signal was perfectly understood – the
> young man stepped out, took his snuff and dram, and the
> clerk recorded his name and attestation. They were then
> collected and the King's Bounty Money paid to them.

In that way the regiment came into being and was mustered in
Strathnaver in August the following year (a cairn at Skail marks
the place). It took some time for uniforms and equipment to be
made available to the men and it was not until September that the
regiment was able to move from Inverness to its first posting on
Guernsey under the command of Lieutenant-Colonel Alexander
Halkett. On arrival the 93rd engaged in coastal defence duties – the
danger of French invasion was a real threat – but the signing of
the Treaty of Amiens made it and other regiments redundant. In
September 1802 it received the order to disband and returned

to Leith in six transports, one of which was wrecked, fortunately without loss of life, off North Shields. As the peace proved to be a temporary measure, the regiment was reprieved when war broke out again and it was moved to Ireland; this was to be its home until May 1805, when it prepared to deploy to the West Indies. Once again fate intervened with the French invasion scare, and the regiment was disembarked from the troopships in Queenstown (Cobh) harbour and placed in defensive positions at Mallow.

The change of plan caused by the emergency also had a bearing on the regiment's future. Instead of sailing across the Atlantic it joined the Highland Brigade, which had been raised for service under the command of Lieutenant-General Sir David Baird, one of the best-known and most experienced commanders of the day, who had made his reputation fighting in the Mysore Wars against Tipu Sahib in southern India. One of the conditions of the Treaty of Amiens was that Dutch colonial possessions should be returned, but when hostilities broke out again in 1803 the British government feared that they would lose control of the strategic sea route to India. (At that time ships bound for India travelled around the Cape of Good Hope.) In conditions of great secrecy an army of 7,000 soldiers assembled at Cork: two brigades were formed, one of them designated as the Highland Brigade, which consisted of 71st Highlanders (later 1st Highland Light Infantry), 72nd Highlanders (later 1st Seaforth Highlanders) and 93rd (Sutherland) Highlanders. The second brigade consisted of 24th (later The South Wales Borderers), 38th (later 1st South Staffordshire Regiment) and 83rd (later 1st Royal Ulster Rifles), and the infantry was reinforced by a small number of dragoons plus artillery. Command of the naval force was given to Commodore Sir Home Popham, an old friend of Baird. On 31 August the invasion fleet left for the South Atlantic and following an uneventful voyage arrived in Table Bay on 4 January 1806.

Baird decided on an immediate landing at Lospard's Bay and although there were problems when one of the landing craft over-turned, drowning 36 soldiers, the main force was soon ashore and ready to march on Cape Town. During the advance, Baird's men came under accurate fire from the Dutch irregular militia but when it became apparent that resistance was futile the defenders sued for terms on 10 January. Cape Town fell into British hands and detachments of troops were sent to occupy Simonstown, Muisenberg, Wynberg and Stellenbosch. The recapture of the Cape is not one of the great victories in the history of the British Army – the historian Sir John Fortescue makes little of it and chides Baird for giving prominence to the Highland regiments – but it provided a much-needed boost at a time when military successes were few and far between. The 93rd was destined to remain in South Africa as part of the British garrison until 1814, and during that time it won a high reputation for the men's discipline and general good behaviour. According to the records every man possessed a copy of the Bible and they formed themselves into a congregation for regular worship, using their own funds to support a minister. In *The Book of Scottish Anecdote* there is a pleasing picture of the regiment in South Africa and the excellent impression it created amongst the local population:

> Their expenses were so well regulated, that while contributing to the support of their clergyman, from the savings of their pay, they were enabled to promote that social cheerfulness which is the true attribute of pure religion and of a well-spent life. While too many soldiers were ready to indulge in that vice which, more than any other, leads to crime in the British army, and spent much of their money in liquor, the Sutherland men indulged in the cheerful amusement of dancing; and in their evening

meetings were joined by many respectable inhabitants who were happy to witness such scenes among the common soldiers in the British service. In addition to these expenses, the soldiers regularly remitted money to their relations in Sutherland.

The regiment's South African deployment came to an end in April 1814 when it returned to Plymouth to be strengthened by reinforcements from the 2nd battalion, which had been formed the previous year. The regiment's return to a home station was destined to be short-lived. Once again it was warned to prepare for overseas service, this time in North America as part of a task force which was formed for operational service against the United States of America under the command of Major-General Sir Edward Pakenham, Wellington's brother-in-law. Two years earlier the US had declared war on Britain and attacked over the border into Canada, but this had been countered by a British assault against Washington which had resulted in the destruction of the White House. In those initial stages Britain could not commit large numbers of troops to the fighting in North America, but the defeat of Napoleon in 1814 allowed the government to send additional naval and land forces across the Atlantic to attempt to capture the city of New Orleans and to take control of the River Mississippi. The expedition set sail at the end of November but it quickly ran into trouble as a result of American preparedness – their commander was Major-General Andrew Jackson, a future president – and the onset of winter weather.

For the 93rd the actual fighting proved to be disastrous. The Americans were well entrenched in lines which included high breastworks, which the British artillery failed to breach and when the attack began on 8 January 1815 the British infantrymen were left exposed and unprotected. An officer in the 93rd provided a telling description of the 'most destructive and murderous fire . . . of grape [shot], musquetry, rifle and buckshot along the whole course and length of their line in front, as well as on our left flank'. Undaunted, the 93rd held their line but the heavy fire was too much for them to bear. After the firing subsided it was discovered that 116 men had been killed while 395 were wounded and 81 were listed as missing. Retreat was the only option and the British took it, embarking on their transports to rejoin the naval fleet. Further fighting was prevented by the arrival of a Royal Navy sloop bearing news of the Treaty of Ghent which had ended the war between Britain and the US on Christmas Eve 1814 – two weeks before the Battle of New Orleans was fought. For the regiment it had been a hellish baptism of fire.

TWO

The Long Peace

Following the defeat of Napoleon at Waterloo it would be another 39 years before the army fought again in a major war against a European power. During that time the nation enjoyed four decades of relative peace and apart from the army's involvement in a succession of colonial campaigns it was a time of relative calm and prosperity on the international front. Inevitably, it was also a time when the army suffered from the defence cutbacks that traditionally follow the cessation of major hostilities; it was no different in the post-Napoleonic period that came to be known as the 'long peace'. Although there were occasional 'invasion scares', most notably in 1846 and 1852, when there were fears of a cross-Channel attack from France, the country's main shield continued to be the Royal Navy and the senior service managed to receive most of the available funding. Another consequence was the need to reinforce and police the country's growing colonial empire. For example, the British garrison in Canada was established at 5,000 troops to offset fears that the United States might wish to indulge in territorial aggrandisement, and the policy was proved in 1841–42 when there was a dispute over the Brunswick border, and again in 1845–46 when the US and Canada almost came to blows over the Oregon border. Troops were also needed to put down disturbances in Demerara in 1823, Mauritius in 1832 and Ceylon (now Sri Lanka) in 1848. Concern that Maoris would attack European settlers in 1845 led to the garrison in New Zealand being increased to 15,000; troops were used in support of the civil power to maintain order in Australia, and at home in Britain the 1840s saw an increase in political unrest with the army being used to quell agitation by Chartists, early socialists who demanded universal male suffrage, the removal of the property qualification for membership of parliament and the re-drawing of electoral districts. Although the movement lacked a central organisation and was largely ineffective, the government took fright at the huge demonstrations it inspired and responded with a heavy hand.

Above all there was also a huge garrison in India, which was needed both to protect the holdings which had been gained in the previous century and to take part in the continuing expansion of the British Raj (British-controlled India). In addition to ill-fated attempts to bring Afghanistan under control in 1838–42, the period saw the annexation of Sind in 1843 and the acquisition of the Punjab following the Sikh Wars of 1845–49. But India was not all just warfare and campaigning. Throughout the nineteenth century and until India became independent in 1947 following the partition with Pakistan, the country was very much a home-from-home for the regiments of the British Army. Compared with service in the United Kingdom, life in India for a soldier was 'cushy'. Even the youngest or most recently enlisted private was treated as a 'sahib' and British soldiers were generally excused the kind of chores which would have been given to them at home in Britain. Cleaning up barracks was left to the sweepers, Indians did all the work in the cookhouse and the laundry was in the hands of the washer-women. In return a number of words entered the soldiers' vocabulary, to be anglicised and used wherever a regiment was posted – buckshee (free, gratis), charpoy (bed), chit (written message), jeldi (hurry up), pukka (proper), tiffin (lunch or midday meal). Many are still in use and can be heard being used by British soldiers in the twenty-first century. Apart from taking part in internal security duties or fighting the occasional war on the frontiers against native opposition, the pattern of service for most soldiers was undemanding and mostly pleasant. Due to the excessive heat, especially during the dry season (April to October) all parades were over by mid-morning and there was no further activity until the cool of the evening. As most British soldiers discovered, once experienced – India is a country which assaults all the senses, often simultaneously – men never forgot the country or its fantastic sights, sounds and smells. Throughout the Victorian period it was not uncommon for soldiers to transfer to other regiments when their own regiments in India returned to Britain.

91ST HIGHLANDERS

At the end of the war against Napoleonic France the 91st remained in France as part of the army of occupation, but it was not the end of its excitements. During the march on Paris two soldiers were killed by French picquets at Cambrai but the regiment had the satisfaction of seeing one of its men, William Ballantine, become one of the first British soldiers to enter the French capital under a flag of truce. The regiment was deployed on internal security duties in the Paris area and did not return until 3 November 1818, when it crossed over to Dover before moving on to Ireland early in the following year.

Although this was a relatively quiet period in Ireland's history – an Act of Union had made the country part of the United

Kingdom in 1801 – the calm was only on the surface. The clamouring for Catholic emancipation was growing in strength and would be strengthened further by the creation of the Catholic Association in 1823 and the emergence of the radical lawyer Daniel O'Connell. In the previous year there had been one of the periodic outbreaks of famine which brought death and hardship to countless families. One visitor to the country, the novelist Sir Walter Scott, noted in his diary: 'Their poverty has not been exaggerated: it is on the verge of extreme human misery.' Faced by political grievance and the horrors of periodic famine, it was not surprising that the people of Ireland nursed grievances that would erupt into outbreaks of trouble throughout the century and into the twentieth century.

After three years in Ireland the regiment crossed the Atlantic to begin a nine-year deployment in the West Indies. For many of the British regiments which served in the area the posting could often be a death sentence. Disease was rampant, particularly yellow fever, and the prospect was not helped by the indifferent living conditions. During the ten-year stay in the Caribbean the regiment lost 20 officers, 30 sergeants and 576 other ranks to yellow fever. In the first year, 1822, the death toll was 152. Some idea of the problems facing regiments in the West Indies can be found in the fact that it took 11 years to repair the condemned barracks at Orange Grove in Trinidad and 20 years to build new barracks at Fort Charlotte in the Bahamas. In an attempt to address this high mortality rate, the War Office introduced a regular rotation of regiments: shorter tours of duty were ordered for the most insalubrious spots and a new pattern of service was introduced, whereby regiments were posted to the Mediterranean for acclimatisation before being sent to the heat and humidity of the West Indies or North America. Later this would be extended to the eastern hemisphere, where regiments spent time in Australia or South Africa before proceeding to India or Ceylon (now Sri Lanka). Between 1839 and 1853 the British Army suffered 58,139 casualties to disease or illness, and contemporary War Office papers reveal that the annual death rates per 1,000 men were 33 for non-commissioned officers and men and 16.7 for officers (in Jamaica it was 69 per 1,000 for officers and men).

In 1831 the regiment sailed back to England for a year before returning to Ireland, where its headquarters were in Mullingar in County Westmeath. By then the Catholic Emancipation Acts had been passed in April 1829 and under its terms all the remaining restrictions debarring Catholics from public office were removed. Not only was this a victory for common sense – in the previous year O'Connell had won the Clare by-election and as a Catholic could not otherwise have sat in parliament – but it also showed that change could be brought about by non-violent means. As a result the following decade was relatively peaceful in Ireland and the 91st's period of duty in the country was without incident, with the regimental diaries recording little of serious interest.

That absence of any action could have made the tour difficult – time hanging heavily on soldiers' hands is never easy for a regiment – but, fortunately, there were opportunities for service overseas. Between 1836 and 1842 a detachment of three companies from the 91st provided the infantry element for the British garrison on the island of St Helena. This was important for two reasons: the island was used as a staging post on the sea route to India and it was the place to which Napoleon had been exiled following his final defeat at Waterloo. Although the former French emperor had died in 1821 his body had not been repatriated to France and was buried in an embalmed state on St Helena. The British government felt it was prudent to provide a small garrison of infantry and artillery to guard the island in case Napoleon's supporters attempted to retrieve the body and return it to France.

At the same time there was growing clamour in France for the body to be given back to the nation so that it could be re-interred in French soil. This was given impetus during the reign of King Louis Philippe and in 1840 the British foreign secretary, Lord Palmerston, agreed to the return of the body with full military ceremony. On 8 October two French warships, the frigate *Belle Poule* and the corvette *La Favorite*, arrived at St Helena's Jamestown Harbour where they were joined by the brig *Oreste* and the British schooner HMS *Dolphin*. Following discussions between the Prince de Joinville, leader of the French delegation, and the British authorities the exhumation was fixed for the following week, exactly 25 years since Napoleon had set foot on the island. The operation to exhume the body began at midnight, with the 91st providing an officers' guard over the tomb. The night was wet and windy and it took time to get into the sarcophagus to reveal the coffin, which was found to have three layers, the final one containing the embalmed and still preserved body within a winding sheet. Prayers were said by the Abbé Coquereau and the resulting scene was captured for posterity by the novelist William Makepeace Thackeray, writing under his journalistic nom-de-plume of Michael Angelo Titmarsh:

> On arriving at the entrance of the town, the troops of the garrison and the militia formed in two lines as far as the extremity of the quay. According to the order for mourning prescribed for the English army, the men had their arms reversed and the officers had crape on their arms, with their swords reversed. All the inhabitants had been kept away from the line of march, but they lined the terraces commanding the town, and the streets were occupied only by the troops, the 91st Regiment being on the right and the militia on the left. The cortège advanced slowly between two ranks of soldiers to the sound of a

funeral march, while the cannons of the forts were fired, as well as those of the 'Belle Poule' and the 'Dolphin'; the echoes being repeated a thousand times by the rocks above James Town. After two hours' march the cortège stopped at the end of the quay, where the Prince de Joinville had stationed himself at the head of the officers of the three French ships of war. The greatest official honours had been rendered by the English authorities to the memory of the Emperor – the most striking testimonials of respect had marked the adieu given by St. Helena to his coffin; and from this moment the mortal remains of the Emperor were about to belong to France.

The accompanying French party was greatly impressed by the firing of a royal salute and the full military honours provided by the 91st and the dignified proceedings did much to heal the breach between the two countries. Napoleon's final resting place was in a magnificent tomb beneath the dome of Hotel des Invalides in Paris.

While these momentous events were taking place, the regiment had sent another detachment of three companies to join the British garrison in South Africa. Based in Cape Colony, they arrived in the aftermath of the Sixth Kaffir War (1834–35). This succession of nine conflicts with the Xhosa people, cattle-raising tribes of Eastern Natal, came about as the result of European expansionism as Dutch settlers began moving eastwards from the Cape in the 1770s. (In later times the word 'kaffir', a corruption of 'Xhosa' developed as a result of the British soldiers' inability to pronounce the Bantu click represented by the 'X', acquired a pejorative meaning; the conflicts are also known as the Cape Frontier Wars.) Because the Dutch attempted to create settlements this led to fighting along the Great Fish River and they turned to the British in Cape Province for help. The use of superior force helped to settle the issue after a fifth war was fought in 1817, but the British military build-up led to increased strains not only with the Xhosa but also with the Dutch. In 1834, attacks on European settlements forced the British governor, Sir Benjamin D'Urban, to drive back the Xhosa over the Great Fish River into a new settlement known as Queen Adelaide Province, where the Dutch were offered compensation for the loss of land. However, by then the Dutch and the British were unwilling to cooperate – incoming missionaries from Britain disliked the Dutch attitudes towards the native Africans – and so began the 'Great Trek' north which allowed the Dutch to create the new province of Natal and, in time, the Orange Free State. The Xhosa forces were led by a tribal chief called Macomo and never numbered more than 7,000 but they proved to be spirited fighters, many of whom possessed firearms. During the course of the operations in Natal there were also heightened tensions with the Boers, who usually refused to obey instructions on the grounds that they were not British subjects. As we shall see, this arrangement did not solve matters but only created the problems which would lead the British and the Dutch to go to war later in the century.

In 1842 the rest of the 91st arrived in South Africa and in the same year the regiment formed a new Reserve Battalion from the depot companies in County Kildare. Most of the men came from other regiments serving in Ireland, notably 146 from the 75th Foot (later 1st Gordon Highlanders), 40 from the 90th Perthshire Light Infantry (later 2nd Scottish Rifles) and over 300 from English and Irish regiments. Originally it was supposed to supply drafts for the regiment in South Africa, as the 2nd battalion had done during the fighting against Napoleon, but there seems to have been an unwillingness on the part of the War Office to formalise the arrangement by reviving the disbanded battalion. Instead it was decided to send the new formation to South Africa to join the 91st, and 540 officers men were despatched under the command of Lieutenant-Colonel M.T.G. Lindsay, formerly of the 78th Highlanders (later 2nd Seaforth Highlanders) on board the *Abercrombie Robinson*, a relatively modern ship of 1,415 tons which was on charter to the War Office. Also on board were detachments of the 27th Foot (later 1st Royal Inniskilling Fusiliers) and the Cape Mounted Rifles as well as 100 women and children.

Following an uneventful voyage, the ship put into Table Bay on 25 August and anchored in shallow water near the mouth of the Salt River. Despite appeals by the harbour-master, who was concerned about the shallow depth of the anchorage, the captain of the *Abercrombie Robinson* did not move his ship into deeper water, and this decision led to disaster three days later when the bay was hit by a huge storm. In the high winds the ship was driven inexorably towards the shore and was soon in grave danger of breaking up. A number of attempts to get a line ashore failed but eventually one of the cutters managed to get through the surf and two large surf boats hauled by oxen were launched to begin the rescue operation. Under the direction of the senior officer present, Captain Bertie Gordon of the 91st (Colonel Lindsay and other officers had disembarked on arrival), orders were given that the evacuation would proceed in the following order: women, children and sick, the detachments of the 27th, the Cape Mounted Rifles and the Reserve Battalion of the 91st, with the companies drawing lots to determine the final order of disembarkation. All soldiers were ordered to parade on the upper deck, fully armed and carrying their knapsacks and great coats. Once the women and children were safely off the stricken ship the soldiers followed, 30 at a time, and the wholesale rescue had been effected by late afternoon. The last to leave was a party of ship's officers and crew under Gordon's command. All told, 700 made good their escape shortly before the *Abercrombie Robinson* broke up in the increasingly heavy swell. In his report Gordon commended the men for not losing their nerve under difficult and demanding circumstances:

> It would be difficult to praise sufficiently the steady discipline of that young and newly formed battalion, thus severely tested during seventeen hours of danger; above eight of which were hours of darkness and imminent peril. That discipline failed not, when the apparent hopelessness of our situation might have led to scenes of confusion and crime. The double guards and sentries which had at first been posted over the wine and spirit stores, were found unnecessary, and they were ultimately left to the ordinary protection of single sentries.

It was an astonishing achievement, and the Reserve Battalion's coolness under pressure was repeated in another troopship involving the 91st ten years later. While carrying around 500 soldiers, with their wives and families and a crew of 132, the *Birkenhead* struck a reef in Simon's Bay off the southern African coast on the night of 26 February 1852. It took just under half an hour for the ship to sink and in that time the women and children were able to escape by lifeboat thanks to the selfless discipline of the soldiers on board, who lined up as if on parade under the command of Lieutenant-Colonel Seton of the 74th Highlanders and kept their places even when all was lost. At the subsequent court martial Captain (later Colonel) Edward Wright of the 91st provided such a graphic account of the tragedy and the soldiers' response to it that King Frederick William IV of Prussia ordered it to be read aloud to his regiments as an example of grace under pressure:

> The order and regularity that prevailed on board, from the moment the ship struck till she totally disappeared, far

exceeded anything that I had thought could be effected
by the best discipline; and it is the more to be wondered
at seeing that most of the soldiers were but a short time in
the service. Everyone did as he was directed and there was
not a murmur or cry amongst them until the ship made
her final plunge – all received their orders and carried
them out as if they were embarking instead of going to the
bottom – I never saw any embarkation conducted with so
little noise or confusion.

Of the 91st's draft of 52 officers and men, 43 were drowned in the
accident and the total death toll was 438, all soldiers or crew of
the *Birkenhead*. Two other Scottish regiments were involved in the
incident: 73rd (later 2nd Black Watch) and 74th Highlanders.

The drafts of men on board *Birkenhead* were needed to reinforce
the garrison at a time when fighting had again broken out with
the Xhosa people. The first of the conflicts, the Seventh Kaffir War,
began in 1846. It was also known as the War of the Axe because
it was sparked by a Xhosa who murdered his escort while being
taken to Grahamstown charged with stealing an axe. When the
murderer refused to surrender to the authorities military action was
threatened, but the incident was used as a pretext for re-opening
the conflict with the Xhosa following a British decision to rescind
D'Urban's creation of Queen Adelaide Province. The new governor,
Sir Peregrine Maitland, was convinced that the Xhosa people had
to be brought under control and their land annexed, and the axe
incident provided the excuse for a pre-emptive strike by moving
against the Xhosa chief, Sandile. However, this time military action
did not produce the expected decisive result as the Xhosa had
learned to avoid pitched battles and turned instead to guerrilla
tactics. During this phase of the conflict the 91st was involved in the
main action at Fort Peddie, which lay between East London and

Port Elizabeth halfway between the Great Fish and Keiskamma rivers. On 28 March 1846 Fort Peddie was attacked by a force of 8,000 Xhosa, and if it had fallen Grahamstown would have come under threat. Heavy artillery fire stopped the attack before it began, but the Xhosa were able to drive off large numbers of cattle from the Mfengu tribe, which was friendly to the British.

Following the action, which both sides counted as a victory – the British because they had forced their assailants to break off the attack and the Xhosa because they had enriched themselves – the Xhosa made for the fastnesses of the Amatola Mountains. It was a good decision. They were accustomed to the hard environment whereas the pursing British infantrymen were dressed in uncomfortable uniforms and encumbered with equipment which was more suitable for campaigning in Europe than fighting a bush war in Africa. Shortage of water was also a problem, and there were additional difficulties when the Xhosa started setting fire to the surrounding mountainsides. In the memoirs of the regiment's medical officer, William Munro, later of the 93rd, to which he transferred in 1854, and later still Surgeon-General, there is a telling description of the difficulties facing the Highlanders and how they tried to overcome them:

> They could march from sunrise to sunset and though without food and *other* refreshment during all that time, not a man fell out of the ranks, so great was their *staying* power, their endurance; and they never got footsore or leg weary, for their feet were as hard as horn, and their muscles like whipcord. The only thing they appeared to dislike was a long halt during the march, for their old muscles got stiff, and would not relax again until they got quickly over a mile or two. Never since those days, and I have passed years of active service, and had much experience since then, have

THE LONG PEACE

I seen soldiers march better than the old 91st – 'the drunken auld deevils', as they called themselves.

Despite being able to cope with the conditions, the 91st made little contact with the opposition and rarely saw the Xhosa at close range. Ammunition was also in short supply, a result of the long lines of communication. Heavy rains then added to the difficulties for both sides and the fighting slumped into stalemate. In an attempt to end the war the following year, 1847, the Xhosa offered to return some cattle and to surrender some arms but this was rejected by the British and campaigning began again in the mountains. In one incident the Reserve Battalion was confronted by a force of 2,000 tribesmen on a position known as the Amatola Flats and lost three men killed and three wounded. A few months later, in September, the Xhosa sued for peace and as part of the agreement were moved into land between the Keiskamma and Kei rivers. The end of hostilities meant that the 91st was able to return to Britain in 1848 – its final destination was Ireland – while the Reserve Battalion remained in South Africa. With them the 91st took Colonel Lindsay, who had been remarkably inefficient during his period in command – the 1848 Annual Inspection Report noted that 'due attention has not been paid to the cleanliness and comfort of the men's messing' and concluded that it was 'slovenly under arms'. Lindsay had also maintained a ridiculous feud with Captain Gordon over non-payment of funds in the wake of the loss of the *Abercrombie Robinson* and at one point threatened to have him court-martialled. Gordon returned home on sick leave in 1845 and later became a distinguished commanding officer of the regiment.

By then a new British governor had arrived in the shape of Lieutenant-General Sir Harry Smith, who had come to the fore as a soldier during the Peninsula campaign and had caused a sensation by marrying a 14-year-old Spanish heiress, Juana Maria de Los

Dolores de Leon, following the capture of Badajoz in 1812. Later he served in India and South Africa, becoming the first governor of Queen Adelaide Province. However, his undoubted military talents were often eclipsed by an excitable nature and an appalling temper, character traits which frequently led him into trouble. On becoming governor he insulted the Xhosa leader Macomo and his fellow chiefs by making them kiss his boots and addressing them as his 'children'. He also succeeded in outraging the Boers by annexing the land beyond the Orange River and making an enemy of their leader, Andries Pretorious. This led to a new round of fighting, which opened in the summer of 1848.

Smith's response was to subdue this fresh threat with a show of strength. He established a reward for the arrest of Pretorious and gathered together a composite force consisting of companies from the 45th Foot (later 1st Sherwood Foresters), 91st Reserve Battalion and 95th Rifles backed up by the Cape Mounted Rifles, and marched them rapidly from Grahamstown to Colesberg. From there he crossed the Orange River and headed for Winberg, the main centre of Boer resistance. The only action took place at Boemplats on 29 August, where a spirited bayonet charge led by the 91st put the enemy to flight. Having won the battle, Smith proclaimed British sovereignty north of the Orange River and returned with his forces to Cape Town. Two years of peace followed but hostilities broke out again at the end of 1850 with another Xhosa uprising in the Amatola Mountains and the situation was exacerbated by unrest amongst the Hottentot people, who had hitherto been loyal allies. This fighting lasted until 1853 and for the men of the 91st Reserve Battalion it was marked by long marches undertaken by British soldiers in the inhospitable uplands they had come to know so well since arriving in South Africa. Once again they played a conspicuous part and suffered numerous casualties: according to an account in the regimental records one of those taken prisoner by the Xhosa was found to have been crucified. It was not until 1855 that the men of the 91st Reserve Battalion returned to Ireland, where they resumed their pre-war duties of supplying drafts to the 1st battalion. With them they took the heartfelt thanks of their senior commander, Lieutenant-General the Hon. Sir George Cathcart, ringing in their ears:

> The field of glory opened to them in a Kaffir War and Hottentot rebellion is possibly not so favourable and exciting as that which regular warfare with an open enemy in the field affords, yet the unremitting exertions called for in hunting well-armed yet skulking savages through the bush and driving them from their innumerable strongholds, are perhaps more arduous than those required in regular warfare and call more constantly for individual exertion and intelligence. The British soldier, always cheerfully obedient to the call, well knows that, when he has done his duty, he is sure to obtain the thanks and good opinion of his gracious Queen.

93RD HIGHLANDERS

At the conclusion of the disastrous Louisiana campaign the 93rd was taken north to Canada, where it embarked at St John's Newfoundland for the transatlantic crossing back to Britain. Its destination was Cork, where it proceeded into barracks at Birr to await reinforcements – 30 sergeants, 11 drummers and 303 other ranks – from the recently disbanded 2nd battalion. Between then and 1818 it was able to send detachments to Athlone, Nenagh and Limerick before moving to Dublin. Marching from one station to another was a taxing business and as the regimental records make clear, it took its toll on the men:

On the march the men carried all their possessions, and while with the ammunition carts, bayonets were fixed all the way, making it very fatiguing. Some got blistered feet, but I have seen a man in great pain refuse to ride, or put his pack on the cart. It was considered unmanly and unsoldierlike to do so. Soap mixed with whisky was a favourite remedy for blistered feet.

During this period the establishment of the 93rd was 45 sergeants, 22 drummers and 800 rank and file, a reduction of some 20 per cent on its wartime footing. As had been the case with the 91st, the regiment arrived in Ireland at a time of growing demands for Catholic emancipation. While this did not erupt into violence at any time and the regiment was spared any involvement in internal security duties, there was one notable confrontation with the local population in Mullingar in 1823. Taunted by 'defiance and insults' a party of 60 soldiers took the matter into their own hands and set off into the town to beat up their tormentors. Although this caused uproar the men were exonerated and the regiment's reputation remained intact.

The deployment came to an end in November 1823, when the 93rd marched to Cobh to board four transports bound for the Windward and Leeward Islands in the Caribbean. Although the 93rd suffered casualties throughout its deployment, the number of deaths was considerably lower than in many other regiments, mainly because the commanding officer, Lieutenant–Colonel Duncan McGregor, was a stickler for maintaining high standards of self–discipline and took a deep interest in his soldiers' welfare. He insisted that each man should possess a Bible and be able to read it and to that end introduced reading classes and encouraged the creation of an environment in which abstinence was not considered unusual. As he told his sister in a letter written from Antigua on 30 March 1830:

The cause of default is invariably rum – rum – rum, and poor fellows they have strong temptations to it, independently of its extreme cheapness. They are induced to drink from the exhilarating effect it produces on their spirits, depressed by the nature of the climate, and, frequently, too, from the derangement of their stomachs being temporarily relieved by rum; but I do hope that the fruits of our schools are now being reaped.

During its ten-year deployment the regiment lost 302 officers and men to disease, mainly yellow fever. The years in the West Indies came to an end in April 1834, when the regiment embarked on the transports *Orestes* and the *Marquis of Huntly* for passage to Ramsgate where on arrival it moved into barracks at Canterbury. The records show that on the return to England only 371 officers and men remained on the active list, 323 were discharged as invalids and 117 decided to stay on in the area by transferring to other regiments. A highlight of the regiment's return was the presentation of new colours by Field Marshal the Duke of Wellington. Following the ceremonial the regiment entertained its august guest to dinner and this was followed by performances by the band and the regimental pipers. Even Colonel McGregor relaxed his regime, allowing 'an allowance of porter' to be provided for the men. According to a report in the *Kentish Observer* of 9 October, the regiment did not stint in its celebrations:

> Carts, laden with roasted and baked meats, were entering the barracks from every part of the neighbourhood where accommodation could be afforded for cooking them. The orderly demeanour of the men, the unassuming deportment of the women, and the neat and cleanly appearance of the children, made a powerful impression upon all who

witnessed the scene . . . and ere evening closed in, the soldiers in small parties, in various portions of the yard, danced the Highland reel to the inspiring strains of the bagpipes.

The following day the 93rd left Canterbury and marched north to Lancashire, where it established headquarters at Blackburn with other companies at Bolton, Rochdale and Burnley. Later it moved its headquarters to Liverpool, with companies at Wigan, Haydock and Chester. This was a prelude to a return to Ireland in October 1836, when it was initially based in Dublin before proceeding to Newry and Downpatrick to provide aid to the civil power. While the regiment was in Armagh it received notice that it should prepare itself once more for foreign service, the most likely destination being Gibraltar. However, before the deployment could take place trouble flared in Canada, forcing the authorities to request military assistance. The revolt was petty enough and confined to the area around Montreal – it was prompted by disagreements over the legislative powers of the assembly and involved mainly French Canadians – but there were fears that the US would take advantage of the situation by allowing sympathisers to cross the border and cause trouble. This did in fact happen shortly after the regiment arrived when some 500 Americans assembled on the US side of the border near Kingston. During the confrontation shots were fired and an officer in the 83rd Foot (later 1st Royal Irish Rifles) was killed, forcing the 93rd's Grenadier company to counter-attack before the trouble got out of hand. During the incident a record written by the adjutant Major William Macdonald shows that the 93rd had its first experience of contact with Canadian militiamen wearing Highland uniform:

Before taking leave of Lower Canada, I may mention in a word or two that in one of the towns we met a Glengarry regiment of Militia, hurriedly mustered and sent to the front. There were some fine strapping men amongst them, but they neither knew anything of discipline nor drill, and moreover scarcely any of them could speak English. I was acting Brigade-Major at the time. I had to bring my knowledge of their language [Gaelic] of which I was always proud, to help them along with their drill, and very much pleased the poor fellows were to find that I could give them some instruction and hints in Gaelic.

Later the regiment moved to Toronto, which was to be its home until 1844, when it returned to Montreal before a final deployment in Quebec. In the summer of 1848 the regiment was relieved by the 79th Highlanders and returned to Scotland on board the troopship *Resistance*. During this period the regimental records show that the average age of the soldiers was 24 years and nine months, that the average service was six years and the men's average height was five feet eight and a half inches. As might be expected, the tallest men were the Grenadiers, at five feet ten inches. The youngest man in the regiment was a drummer aged 14, while there were two men aged over 40. Most of the soldiers continued to come from the Highlands and islands, justifying the findings of a War Office report which stated that the 93rd was the most Highland of the official Highland regiments:

Orkney and Shetland: two corporals, five privates
Caithness: four sergeants, seven corporals, 69 privates
Sutherland: five sergeants, two corporals, 48 privates
Ross and Cromarty: four sergeants, three corporals,
    39 privates

Inverness: two sergeants, one corporal, one drummer,
45 privates

Nairn: one drummer, 11 privates

Moray: one sergeant, two corporals, one drummer,
36 privates

Perthshire: one sergeant, one corporal, one drummer,
40 privates.

At the same time four sergeants, one drummer and 68 privates came from Aberdeen, while two drummers and 32 privates came from Lanarkshire. Only five privates were listed as being English and only two privates were Irish. Prior to enlistment 212 admitted to having a trade, the most numerous, 64, being weavers, while 379 had worked on the land as labourers or farm servants. Around half of the men were Gaelic speakers.

THREE

The Crimean War and
the Indian Mutiny

In the middle of the nineteenth century the people of Britain were forced to confront two crises which struck at the heart of their confidence in the country's armed forces and the whole institution of empire. The first was the war against Russia, which was fought in the Crimea and the Baltic and in which Britain's allies were France, the Ottoman Empire and Sardinia; the second was the Indian Mutiny, which broke out in the Ganges Valley a year later. Neither was connected in any strategic sense but both rattled the harmony of Victorian life and led to widespread changes in the way the army was organised. Only the 93rd Highlanders took part in both campaigns and it gained great distinction by winning seven Victoria Crosses, the new medal for supreme gallantry which was instituted by Queen Victoria in January 1856 to honour 'most conspicuous bravery, or some daring or pre-eminent act of valour or self-sacrifice or extreme devotion to duty' (see Appendix). During the period of the two campaigns, 1854–59, the 91st spent most of the time serving as garrison troops in Greece and at Corfu, which came into British hands at the end of the war with Napoleon (see Chapter Four).

The Crimean War encompassed maladministration and human suffering on a grand scale; disaster marched hand in hand with heroism. It was also the first conflict to be fully covered by the press, most notably by William Howard Russell of *The Times*, and the reports from the front caused national outrage. For the British there was the heroic myth created by Tennyson's well-known poem 'The Charge of the Light Brigade' and the atonement offered by the example of Florence Nightingale and her gallant company of nurses in the infamous military hospital at Scutari. There was, though, more to the war than the oft-rehearsed catalogue of blunders redeemed by basic human courage and a refusal to surrender to overwhelming odds. For all the participants the war ended the long peace of 1815 and set in train the succession of small European conflicts and power struggles which dominated the second half of the nineteenth century and which would eventually lead to the global war of 1914–18.

The conflict had its starting point as a petty squabble between the Orthodox and Catholic churches over the rights to the holy sites in Jerusalem – the actual spark was possession of the key to the main door of the Church of the Nativity in Bethlehem – and quickly spread to become a war to prevent Russian expansionist ambitions in the Black Sea geo-strategic region. Tsar Nicholas I entertained hopes of using a perceived weakness of Ottoman rule to gain influence in the Balkans, where there was a significant Slav population, and began exerting diplomatic and military pressure on Constantinople. Matters escalated relentlessly and quickly brought the main participants to the verge of war. In the summer of 1853 Russian forces invaded the Ottoman Danubian principalities of Moldavia and Wallachia (modern Romania), a move which forced Turkey to declare war in October. From that point onwards a general conflict became inevitable, as both Britain and France were opposed to the Russian moves and wished to shore up Ottoman rule. At the beginning of 1854 a Turkish naval squadron was overwhelmed and destroyed by the Russian fleet at Sinope, and a few weeks later the British and French fleets sailed into the Black Sea followed by the mobilisation of both countries' land forces.

THE CRIMEAN WAR: 93ᴿᴰ HIGHLANDERS

War was eventually declared at the beginning of April and command of the British expeditionary force was given to Lord Raglan who, as Lord Fitzroy Somerset, had been Wellington's military secretary in the Peninsula and who had an unblemished, if unspectacular, military career. His connection to Wellington counted for much, as did his personal courage (he lost his right arm at Waterloo) and his ability to get on with the French allies (he spoke fluent French but discommoded his allies in the Crimea by referring to them as 'the enemy').

On the force's departure *The Times* called it 'the finest army that has ever left these shores', but it soon became clear that the encomium was misplaced. No one doubted the courage of the soldiers who went to war with the cheers of their fellow countrymen ringing in their ears, but the direction of the war was soon revealed as a shambles. Amongst Raglan's force was a Highland Brigade which was under the command of Brigadier-General Sir Colin Campbell, a brilliant soldier, but of modest means, who had started his career with the 8ᵗʰ Foot (later The King's Liverpool Regiment) in the Peninsula and had come to prominence fighting in the Sikh Wars of 1845–46 and 1848–49. The other regiments in the brigade were 42ⁿᵈ (Royal Highland) Regiment and the 79ᵗʰ (Cameron) Highlanders; the brigade served in the 1ˢᵗ Division, commanded by HRH The Duke of Cambridge, a cousin of Queen Victoria who later became commander-in-chief of the British Army. (A stickler for good form and discipline, he was contemptuous of educated soldiers, once telling a fellow officer: 'Brains! I don't believe in brains. You haven't any, I know, sir!') At the time, the 93rd was under the command of Lieutenant-Colonel Ainslie and numbered 34 officers, 107 non-commissioned officers, 21 drummers and 950 soldiers. On 27 March they embarked for the Black Sea on board the troopship *Himalaya*, but by the time the British and French forces arrived in the principalities in mid-June the Russians had withdrawn from the area following an aggressive deployment by the Austrian army. To compound the muddle, there was a cholera epidemic in the allied armies and within weeks of landing in the principalities they had suffered 10,000 casualties. (The 93rd lost 54 dead and over 400 were badly affected.) With public confidence in the enterprise waning, the decision was taken to attack and destroy the large Russian naval base at Sevastopol on the south-western side of the Crimean peninsula. For the allied armies this meant landing near Eupatoria to the north and attacking down the coastline towards Sevastopol, the idea being to gain the objective before winter set in.

Although the landing was unopposed, the Russians had brought up their forces under the command of Prince Alexander Sergeevich Menshikov to block the allies' advance towards Sevastopol and the first set-piece battle of the war was fought on the banks of the River Alma on 20 September when the allied and Russian armies collided close to the northern approaches to Sevastopol. The plan of action was the brain-child of the French commander, Marshal Leroy de Saint-Arnaud, and while it was straightforward, it left little room for manoeuvre. With both armies drawn up on opposing fronts, the French were directed to engage the Russians on the left flank towards the high ground at the river mouth while the British would attack from the centre. If the pincer movement succeeded, the Russians would be prevented from withdrawing and their lines of reinforcement and supply would be cut off. It was decided that the French 2nd Division would form the vanguard and advance at 5 a.m. the next morning, followed by the remaining allied divisions two hours later. Covering fire would be provided by the warships lying off the coast.

Dawn the following day brought only confusion, and the timetable dictated by the French had to be altered because the British forces were in no position to move off at the agreed hour. However, this was not due to any tardiness on the part of the British. Aware that the baggage train and reserve supplies had to be protected, Raglan had ordered part of the army to face east to prevent a possible flank attack, and it took time for such a large force to wheel round into the line of march. The growing heat also added to the difficulties faced by the infantrymen, sweating beneath their colourful red or green uniform jackets and the equally exotic headwear of ostrich-feathered caps and rigid shakos.

The delay caused the French to halt – they used the time to brew up mid-morning coffee – and it was not until 10.30 a.m. that the allied army was able to advance on a broad front towards the River Alma. Ahead of them lay a landscape that might have been created for warfare. Taking full advantage of the high, narrow escarpment above the winding river, the Russian field commander, Prince Menshikov, had concentrated his forces on the slopes of Kourgané Hill, which dominated the road to Sevastopol. On the shoulder above the village of Bourliuk two fortified earthworks – known as the Greater and Lesser Redoubts – had been constructed for use by artillery and infantry. This was the centrepiece of the Russian defences: the allies would be obliged to cross the river and press home their attack against well-defended positions on higher ground.

Only to the west had Menshikov left matters to chance but, even so, he clearly thought that his assumptions were correct. Here the escarpment gave way to 350-foot sheer cliff faces flanking the river, and so steep and barren were they that Menshikov believed them to be inaccessible. As it was dead ground, only one regiment and a few guns were deployed, Menshikov having reasoned that no commander in his senses would commit men to a difficult assault against such a precipitous position. Later he claimed not to have known – but should have taken the trouble to discover, given the fact that the Russians were fighting on home ground – that there was a narrow path up the cliff face and that the approaches were by no means impregnable to determined troops. That lack of foresight was to cost the Russians the battle.

But as Menshikov and his staff watched the allied armies halt one mile short of the river they were confident that the expected assault would be stopped in its tracks, secure in the knowledge that they held the high ground and that it would be up to the enemy to dislodge them. Indeed, so carefree was the moment that the Russians had allowed a party of Sevastopol's prominent citizens to take a picnic to the battlefield so that they could watch the expected defeat of the allied forces. From a hastily improvised grandstand on Telegraph Hill they sat in elegant rows, watching the preparations through opera-glasses and with glasses of champagne within easy reach. At the time watching battles was a common enough practice, no different from spending a day at the races, and the members of the party, which included women, were in high spirits as they watched the two armies square up to one another across the Alma.

It was a moment which none of them, participants or spectators, would ever forget; yet there was an air of unreality about the preparations in the midday heat as the two allied commanders met to confer. What they said is open to doubt, for neither man recorded the conversation, but from what followed it is clear that Raglan rejected Saint-Arnaud's proposal for a flank attack because his cavalry force was outnumbered and that, therefore, he would be unable to dislodge the Russians. Instead, he decided to press home a frontal assault on Kourgané Hill once the French had engaged the Russians on the right. Shortly after one o'clock the order to advance was sounded and the first units of the allied army moved forward to cross the river. On the British left was the Light Division, supported by the Duke of Cambridge's 1st Division; to the right was the 2nd followed by the 3rd, while the recently arrived 4th Division supplied the reserve together with the cavalry. To their left the French advanced steadily towards Telegraph Hill and started scaling the perpendicular path which Menshikov had unwisely chosen to ignore.

While the French pressed home their attack the British divisions were forced to play a waiting game, Raglan having decided that it would be foolhardy to begin the assault until his allies had made sufficient progress. In any other circumstances it should have been a welcome respite, a quiet moment before battle was joined, but for the patient ranks of infantrymen Raglan's order provided many of them with their first taste of action. While green-tunicked riflemen engaged Russian skirmishers on the river banks, the Russian artillery on Kourgané Hill fired their first rounds into the unprotected ranks of the 2nd and the Light Division. Having deployed from column into line the infantry, drawn up by battalion, made a tempting target, and the Russian heavy gunners took advantage of it. According to the historian A. W. Kinglake, who was present and who managed to remain in contact with most of the commanders during this first phase of the battle, the tone was set by Campbell, whose Highland Brigade would attack the heavily defended Russian right. As his men waited under fire and as casualties mounted, he addressed them with 'a few words – words simple, and, for the most part, workmanlike, yet touched with the fire of warlike sentiment':

Now, men, you are going into action. Remember this:
whoever is wounded – I don't care what his rank is – whoever
is wounded must lie where he falls till the bandsmen come
to attend him. No soldiers must go carrying off wounded
men. If any soldier does such a thing, his name shall be
stuck up in his parish church. Don't be in a hurry about
firing. Your officers will tell you when it is time to open
fire. Be steady. Keep silence, fire low. Now men, the army
will watch us; make me proud of the Highland Brigade!

After much dithering, for it was his first experience of battle, the
Duke of Cambridge committed the Guards Brigade (the other
formation in the 1st Division) and the Highland Brigade into
action at half past three. The attack of the 1st Division provides
the Crimean campaign with one of its many celebrated images.
The Guards regiments, the Grenadiers on the right, Scots Fusilier
Guards in the centre and Coldstreamers on the left, advanced with
a parade-ground precision which would not have disgraced Horse
Guards; while to their left, on the eastern slopes of Kourgané, the
kilted Highlanders pushed ahead with their customary eagerness,
anxious to be in a fight. They represented the cream of the
British Army, the Guards regiments proud of their discipline and
commitment to excellence, the kilted Highlanders jealous of their
reputation as fighting soldiers. The battle was won on the slopes of
Kourgané Hill, where both brigades attacked the Russian positions
with a clinical precision.

By four o'clock the Russian army was in full retreat and the
civilian spectators had long since left the battlefield, according to
Russell, having been obliged 'to fly for their lives in their carriages'.
Menshikov's army was in complete disarray and the first battle to
be fought on the European mainland in half a century was at an
end, scarcely three hours after it had commenced in earnest. It was

a satisfying moment for Raglan, and his first taste of action since he had lost his arm at Waterloo all those years ago. With his staff he left his exposed position and rode over the post road to climb Kourgané Hill to confer with his divisional commanders. At the summit he was greeted by cheering Highlanders, many of whom were meeting their commander for the first time. Carefully averting his eyes from the hill opposite, which was thick with dead and wounded, Raglan thanked Campbell for his work that afternoon. By way of reply the Scottish general asked permission for him and his staff to wear the Highland bonnet in place of the usual cocked hat worn by staff officers, an honour which singled them out from the other brigade commanders. Raglan's eyes filled with tears and he could not speak, but simply nodded his permission. During the fighting the 93rd lost one officer and five soldiers killed, and 30 soldiers wounded.

The Alma marked the end of the mobile phase of the war; ahead lay the lengthy and costly operations to capture Sevastopol. When Raglan first arrived at Balaklava, which was to be the allies' gateway to the Black Sea, he believed that an immediate assault might have taken the city because the Russians were in disarray, but he was overruled by the French. Instead the allies delayed to allow their heavy guns to be brought up and preparations were made for an assault to begin during the second half of October. Unfortunately, when the barrage began on 17 October it made little impression on the heavily defended Russian positions and matters did not improve over the days that followed. Before the month was out, though, the failure of the artillery to breach Sevastopol's defences had been put into perspective by news of an even greater calamity – the first reports of the loss of the Light Brigade on 25 October.

So firmly is this action entrenched in the British consciousness that it is often thought of as a display of pluck and courage rather than as a blunder which should never have happened. Indeed, the charge of the Light Brigade soon came to be regarded as something glorious in its own right, an incident which achieved nothing except the memory of undying heroism; and its story has been told many times, not just by the participants but also by those who observed it. But memorable though it was – for all the wrong reasons – it formed only a small part of the Battle of Balaklava. It also helped to mask two other incidents in which the British got the better of their Russian enemies – the stand of the 93rd against Russian cavalry and the successful charge of the Heavy Brigade.

It was a day that began well but ended badly. In the morning the British forces were on the eastern extremity of the besieging army and their positions to the south of Sevastopol on the heights above Balaklava were exposed to attack by Menshikov's field army. An inner line of defence was formed by Royal Marines and naval artillery, and the outer line on the Causeway Heights was guarded by Turkish troops in hastily constructed earthworks. Beyond them lay the North Valley and Fedukhine Heights, and overlooking the South Valley was a force consisting of the Cavalry Division and a small force of guns of W Battery Royal Artillery, some Turkish infantry and the 93rd Highlanders, all under Campbell's command.

As a defensive deployment it was completely inadequate, and inevitably the Russians took advantage of its failings. A field force under Lieutenant-General Pavel Liprandi consisting of 25,000 infantry, 34 squadrons of cavalry and 78 artillery pieces had been assembled around the village of Chorgun to the north-east of Balaklava. Its objective was relatively simple: to concentrate extreme force on a weak British position and then to threaten Balaklava. The assault began at 6.30 a.m. with an artillery barrage and Liprandi intended to follow it up with a three-pronged attack on the Causeway Heights. At worst a victory would give the Russian forces a tactical advantage; at best it could win the war.

For the first hour or so the battle was an unequal artillery duel between the Russian and Turkish guns. Firing roundshot to devastating effect the Russian 18- and 12-pounders caused terrible damage to the Turkish positions. Soon the Turkish resistance began to crumble as Russian cavalry and infantry moved forward to overwhelm their positions. From his command position on the Sapouné Heights above the Woronzoff Road Raglan saw the advance and sent orders for the 1st and 4th Divisions to move into the South Valley. At the same time the cavalry was ordered into the North Valley to cover Campbell's exposed position. The danger was now apparent. When the Russian cavalry reached the causeway crossroads they could see the British guns but not the 93rd Highlanders, who had taken cover from the artillery fire and were hidden from the Russians' view. This was all that stood between them and Balaklava. For the advancing 400 cavalry troopers it was too good an opportunity to miss and they took full advantage of it.

This was cavalry against infantry (and a few Turkish guns) and its outcome depended on which side won the battle of wills. Everything depended on the resolution of the defenders and the determination of the attackers: if the first held firm there was every chance that infantrymen had little to fear from charging horsemen. Precisely that happened at Balaklava. 'Remember, there is no retreat from here,' Campbell famously told the 93rd. 'You must die where you stand.' To which the Highlanders offered the phlegmatic reply: 'Aye, aye, Sir Colin, and needs be we'll do that.' That said, the Highlanders stood up and opened fire. The first volleys failed to halt the Russian charge, but when they wheeled round to the left in an attempt to outflank the 93rd the close-range fire from the Highlanders' Minié rifles succeeded in driving them off. From the hills above, Russell had a grandstand view and for *The Times* he commemorated the action with words which passed into history:

> The ground flies beneath their [Russian] horses' feet;
> gathering speed at every stride, they dash on towards that
> thin red streak topped with a line of steel. The Turks fire
> a volley at 800 yards, and run. The Russians come within
> 600 yards, down goes that line of steel in front, and out
> rings a thundering volley of Minié musketry. The distance
> is too great; the Russians are not checked, but still sweep
> onwards with the whole force of horse and man, through
> the smoke, here and there knocked over by the shot of our
> batteries above. With breathless suspense every one waits
> the bursting of the wave upon the line of Gaelic rock; but
> ere they come within 150 yards, another volley flashed
> from the levelled fire, and carries death and terror into the
> Russians. They wheel about, open files right and left, and
> fly back faster than they came.

The 'thin red streak' emerged again in 1877 in a revised edition
of Russell's history of the war as the more felicitous 'thin red line'
and the phrase quickly established itself as a cliché of Victorian
jingoism. That should not detract from the original report which,
although somewhat breathless, was written in the excited aftermath
of battle and remains an accurate enough description of the 93rd's
repulse of the Russian charge. Later, Liprandi tried to gloss over
the incident by claiming that a force of British heavy cavalry was
present and assisted in the defence. Certainly, the Heavy Brigade
was in the vicinity but its moment of glory came a few minutes
later in another part of the field, when it broke the Russian 6th
Hussar Brigade.

In the winter that followed the action the 93rd suffered the same
deprivations as the besieging force and lost 88 men to illness and
the bitter cold. Conditions improved in the spring with the arrival
of fresh supplies and hutted accommodation, but by then the war

was in stalemate. In May the 93rd joined the rest of the Highland Brigade (now augmented by the addition of the 71st Highland Light Infantry) in an operation to take the port of Kertch, which covered the Sea of Azov and was an important conduit for supplying Sevastopol. At dawn on 24 May 1855 60 ships of the allied fleet made a rendezvous off Cape Takil, and following a brief bombardment the troops were able to make an unopposed landing. The town fell quickly and, having destroyed the government buildings and an arsenal, the allies were able to march to Yenikale on the other side of the peninsula. There the destruction continued and it was made worse by the pillaging which followed the order to raze any buildings which might be useful to the Russian war effort. Mission accomplished, the brigade returned to renew the efforts to complete the siege of Sevastopol, which finally fell on 8 September. Although the regiment was destined to spend another winter in the Crimea the war was as good as over and diplomacy took over as both sides attempted to broker a peace agreement. The French left first, followed by the British regiments, and each one was met by Queen Victoria, who felt that in some small measure she should thank them personally for their loyal services. The 93rd embarked on 13 June 1856 and arrived in Portsmouth a month later before proceeding to Aldershot. It was not destined to be a long posting. Early the following year the regiment was warned for service in China but then fate intervened to return it to Campbell's command.

THE INDIAN MUTINY: 93RD HIGHLANDERS

In the summer of 1857 there was a serious outbreak of violence in India involving Indian regiments of the East India Company's Bengal Army which rapidly escalated to threaten the whole fabric of British rule. On 10 May, the uprising known as the Indian (or Sepoy) Mutiny began at Meerut, where the 11th and 20th Native

Infantry and 3rd Cavalry regiments rose up against the local European population and started slaughtering them. The trouble had been simmering throughout the year and, amongst other grievances, the flashpoint was the decision to issue Indian troops with cartridges using the grease of pigs and cows, offending both Muslims (who regard pigs as unclean) and Hindus (for whom cows are sacred). The trouble spread to other British garrisons at Cawnpore, where the garrison was slaughtered on 27 June despite promises of safe conduct, and at Lucknow, where the European population was besieged in the Residency by a force of 60,000 mutineers. Reinforcements from Britain were ordered and it was to meet that need that the 93rd departed for India on board the transports *Belleisle* and *Mauritius*, arriving in Calcutta on 20 September, where they were met by Campbell, now a lieutenant-general. Their first destination was Fatehpur, halfway between Benares (Varanasi) and Cawnpore, where they were addressed by Campbell and shown the scene of the massacre which sparked the uprising. William Forbes Mitchell (later Forbes-Mitchell), a sergeant in the 93rd, recorded the general's words in his later account of the mutiny:

> I must tell you, my lads, there is work of difficulty and danger before us – harder work and greater dangers than any we encountered in the Crimea. But I trust to you to overcome the difficulties and to brave the dangers. The eyes of the people at home – I may say the eyes of Europe and the whole of Christendom – are upon us; and we must relieve our countrymen, women and children, now shut up in the Residency of Lucknow . . . So when we make an attack you must come to close quarters as quickly as possible; keep well together, and use the bayonet. Remember that the cowardly Sepoys, who are eager to murder women and children, cannot look a European soldier in the face when

it is accompanied by cold steel. Ninety-third! You are my own lads; I rely on you to do the work!

A voice from the ranks called out, 'Aye, aye, Sir Colin, ye ken us and we you; we'll bring the women and children out o' Lucknow or die wi' you in the attempt!'

Once assembled, the regiment joined the forces which were being assembled to march to relieve the British garrison besieged in Lucknow. Although the first attempt under Brigadier-General Sir Henry Havelock had been successful, it had proved impossible to withdraw the civilian population and the city was once again under siege by the rebels. On 14 November Lucknow was in sight and Campbell finalised his plans to attack the rebel positions. Under his command he had 4,700 soldiers and 49 artillery pieces; against them the defenders numbered 30,000 although not all were trained soldiers. Having left his heavy baggage and stores in the Dilkusha park Campbell ordered the 93rd to make a feinting attack to the left across a canal, but this was beaten back by superior opposition numbers. The next day the main attack began with an assault on the Sikandarbagh, a large fortified palace and garden. During this phase the 93rd successfully secured the left flank by capturing the seria (harem) and barrack buildings. Heavy guns were then brought up and once the walls had been breached three regiments of infantry – 4th Punjab Infantry, 53rd Foot (later 1st King's Shropshire Light Infantry) and 93rd Highlanders – were ordered to storm the building. Amongst those watching the action was a young artillery officer, Frederick Sleigh Roberts (later Field Marshal Lord Roberts VC), who recorded the scene in his memoirs:

A Highlander was the first to reach the goal, and was shot dead as he jumped into the enclosure; a man of the 4th Punjab Infantry came next, and met the same fate. Then followed

Captain [F. W. Traill] Burroughs and Lieutenant Cooper
of the 93rd, and immediately behind them their Colonel
(Ewart), Captain Lumsden of the 30th Bengal Infantry, and
a number of Sikhs and Highlanders as fast as they could
scramble through the opening. A drummer-boy must have
been one of the first to pass that grim boundary between
life and death, for when I got in I found him just inside the
breach, lying on his back quite dead – a pretty-looking fair-
headed lad, not more than fourteen years of age.

Spurred on by Pipe Major John McLeod playing 'The Haughs of
Cromdale' they forced their way into the building amidst shouts
of 'Remember Cawnpore!' and by the end of the afternoon the
Sikandarbagh was in British hands. The next target was the Shah
Najaf mosque, but it fell without resistance. During the assault the
regiment lost two officers and 20 soldiers killed and 68 officers
and men wounded. The total casualties in the attacking force
were 45 officers and 496 soldiers killed or wounded. Mindful of
those losses, Campbell decided against securing Lucknow and
confined his operations to ensuring the safety of the garrison
and the civilians, the first step being to evacuate the women and
children. For the next three days preparations were put in hand to
begin the evacuation, which eventually began at midnight on 22
November with the 93rd providing the rearguard as the column
withdrew towards Cawnpore. En route Campbell received the
alarming news that a huge rebel force numbering 13,000 was in the
vicinity under the leadership of Tatya Tope who had been largely
responsible for the Cawnpore massacre. Although outnumbered
– 4,000 soldiers had been left behind at the Alambagh outside
Lucknow – Campbell engaged the rebels to the west of Cawnpore
with the 93rd Highlanders and the 42nd Royal Highlanders leading
the charge and continuing the pursuit down the Kalpi road. As

the British regiments and their Indian allies swept after the rebels the speed and aggression of the attack caused havoc and all too often, as Forbes Mitchell recalled, the mutineers simply fled as fast as possible from the field. At one stage the 93rd came across stark evidence of the panic:

> The camp was deserted, but no preparations had been made to carry off anything; the tents were all standing, the wagons were unpacked, and the bullocks feeding beside them. Their hospital tents alone were tenanted by the sick and wounded, who, as we passed, held up their hands, and begged for mercy; our men turned from them in disgust, unable to pity but unwilling to strike a wounded foe. The rum was in front of the camps, casks standing on end with the heads knocked off for our convenience, the rebels hoping we would fall upon it and become an easy prey to their columns still drawn up beyond the camp. But the men passed on and the supernumerary ranks soon upset the casks.

On another occasion the Light Company and two other rifle companies occupied a large and comfortable Indian house which was full of looted goods, including a large quantity of wine which the officers ordered to be destroyed. An equally large supply of rose water was also discovered but this was preserved, the records relating that it 'proved most refreshing for bathing purposes'.

The next three months were spent in creating a huge force numbering 25,664 men and consisting of four infantry divisions, one cavalry division, one artillery division and an engineer brigade. By the beginning of March Campbell was ready to attack the mutineers, whose numbers had by then swollen to an estimated 100,000. The subsequent fighting lasted 19 days and involved a good deal of close-quarter fighting before Lucknow was finally recaptured on 21 March. During the operations the 93rd lost two officers and 13 soldiers killed and three officers and 63 soldiers wounded. There was also a seventh award of a Victoria Cross, six having been won earlier at Lucknow (see Appendix) and the attack led to the final defeat of the rebels. On this occasion the coveted medal was awarded to the adjutant, Lieutenant William McBean who had started life as a ploughman in Inverness-shire before joining the army. During his service with the 93rd he was commissioned from the ranks, an unusual occurrence, and according to regimental lore he was a worthy recipient of both the medal and his commission. Earlier in his military career it was suggested to him that he should take aside a bullying corporal and give him a good beating. 'Tutts, mon,' was McBean's reply. 'It wadna do at a'; I am going to command this regiment before I leave it, and 'twad be a bad start to thrash the drill corporal.' McBean was as good as his word and eventually retired from the army in the rank of major-general. Others were less fortunate. Although Captain F.W. Traill Burroughs was one of the first through the breach in the original assault at Lucknow, his courage was not recognised and he nursed a lifelong grievance about the omission. (Campbell had asked the regiment to nominate the recipients by vote and the officers had decided in favour of Captain W.G.D. Stewart as he was 'a popular figure in the regiment'.)

Following the fall of Lucknow and the operations outside Cawnpore, the regiment was brigaded with the 42nd Royal Highlanders and the 79th Cameron Highlanders in the remaining operations to subdue Oudh and was involved in an ill-conceived attack on Fort Ruiya under the overall command of Major-General Robert Walpole, who was described by an accompanying army doctor as 'a great dolt'. Even William Howard Russell was not impressed, telling the readers of *The Times* that he was 'surprised Sir Colin [Campbell] trusts his Highlanders to Walpole'.

The war reporter's reservations were not misplaced. On entering the rebel stronghold of Rohilkhand from the west of Oudh Walpole approached the fort at Ruiya and, without attempting a preliminary reconnaissance, decided on a frontal assault. He even ignored the intelligence gained by a trooper of Hodson's Horse, an Indian cavalry regiment, that the rebel leader Nirput Singh would retire if a show of force was made in front of the walls. During the attack the defenders were able to produce heavy fire as the first assault troops tried to fight their way towards the steep sides of the mud fort. Altogether, Walpole's force sustained six officers and 112 soldiers killed or wounded. Amongst the casualties was Lieutenant-Colonel the Hon. Adrian Hope, a popular officer and a superb soldier, who had commanded the 93rd. His loss was deeply regretted within the regiment: William Munro noted in his memoirs that as Hope was buried he observed 'that on the faces of his men there was a rigid sternness, and from their eyes flashed angry ominous glances as they sought for some *one* on whom to cast the blame of this great sacrifice'.

Despite being written off as 'blundering and obstinate' by Russell, who also reported that the 42nd and the 93rd were 'in a state of furious wrath and discontent with their General' Walpole retained Campbell's confidence and there was better fortune for him when the British defeated a rebel force led by Khan Bahadur Khan outside Bareilly on 5 May. This involved fighting in built-up areas – the city consisted of large numbers of sprawling townships and suburbs – and the actual combat was conducted with a ferocity which surprised the attacking force, led by the Highland Brigade. The defenders were Muslims and they showed that they were prepared to fight to the death. Campbell's response was to order the use of the bayonet, and Bareilly eventually fell two days later. Following the successful outcome, the 93rd remained in Bareilly as a garrison until early in 1859, when it moved north to Simla in the foothills of the Himalayas. Later, a memorial to the 93rd was consecrated in the High Church of St Giles, Edinburgh and it records the regiment's casualties during 'The Mutiny in India': five officers and 45 soldiers killed in action, one officer and 37 soldiers died of wounds, one officer and 83 soldiers died of sickness.

FOUR

Imperial Soldiering

The Crimean War proved to be a watershed in the history of the British Army in that it exposed gross shortcomings in administration and in its aftermath the War Office instituted a number of reforms to improve the lot of the British soldier. Changes were also made to the operation and structure of the army but, given the prevailing conservatism, many of the proposed reforms took time to take root. A Staff College came into being at Camberley to provide further intensive training for promising officers, the Crimean conflict having exposed the weakness of reliance on regimental soldiering alone. Recruitment problems were addressed by introducing short-service enlistment, the number of years being reduced from 21 years to six years with the Colours and six in the Reserves. As for the purchase of officers' commissions, which had been much criticised during the war, the system was not abolished until 1871. On the equipment side the first breech-loading rifles were introduced in 1868 (the Snider followed by the Martini-Henry and the Enfield) but the army's traditional red coats were not replaced by khaki until the 1880s, when campaigning in the deserts of Egypt and Sudan made ceremonial dress inappropriate for operation service. (The change to khaki was gradual and was not made official until 1902.) In appearance the regiments in the Crimea looked remarkably similar to their forebears in the Peninsula.

The terrible conditions endured by the army also encouraged a flurry of interest in soldiers' welfare. In 1857 a Royal Sanitary Commission investigated the conditions in barracks and military hospitals, and its findings merely underlined the nation's low opinion of its armed forces. The mortality rate amongst soldiers was double that of the civilian population, with the home-based army losing 20.8 per cent of its strength due to illness or disease. The Commissioners placed the blame on unsanitary conditions, poor diet and the 'enervating mental and bodily effects produced by ennui'. Their recommendations led to a steady improvement in the soldier's lot: a programme was instituted to improve ventilation, sanitary conditions and waste disposal in British barracks and steps were taken to provide soldiers with better leisure facilities in an attempt to cut down on the scourge of drunkenness. Two years later parliament voted £726,841 for the improvements, but the reforms proved to be a slow and expensive process and it was to take until 1861 before the Commission on Barracks and Hospitals could report that 45 barracks had proper lavatories in place of the usual cesspits, which had been there for generations. One other major change only affected the Highland regiments such as the 93rd: in 1854 the War Office finally sanctioned the official employment of a pipe-major and five pipers. Previously they had been listed as drummers in order to receive the additional extra-duty pay of one penny a day, but the ruling did not apply to non-Highland regiments or to the Lowland regiments, where the pipers were paid for by the officers' mess. (In 1850 the 91st was expressly forbidden by the War Office to employ pipers.) The mutiny in India also prompted reform: in its aftermath steps were taken to increase the size of the garrison in the sub-continent to ensure that the Indian army of 190,000 soldiers was balanced by the presence of 80,000 British soldiers.

For the next 60 years Britain was to play no part in the wars which were fought in Europe, the main conflict being the Franco–Prussian War of 1871. Instead, the army was to spend most of its time engaged in colonial police-keeping duties in various parts of Britain's imperial holdings. The 91st and the 93rd were both part of that process.

91ST FOOT

While the 93rd had been fighting in the Crimea and in India, the 91st had been stationed in Greece and the Ionian islands as part of a British and French initiative to deter any Russian interest in the area. It was considered to be a plum posting. The territory had come into British possession in 1815 as a result of the Treaty of Paris which had concluded the Napoleonic War, and was ruled as the United States of the Ionian Islands with its capital on the island of Corfu, the seat of the British Lord High Commissioner. Although the arrangement provided an excellent and easy-going administration – cricket was introduced and is played by Corfiotes to this day – there were also calls for the islands to be returned to Greece and these had led to outbreaks of trouble from 1848 onwards. As a result, the British government despatched a mission led by Henry Bulwer Lytton, the Colonial Secretary and the author of *The Last Days of Pompeii*, but he tended to view the problem through the prism of classical Greece and it was not until 1858 that further moves were made to solve the problem through the appointment of William Ewart Gladstone as Lord High Commissioner Extraordinary. During the deployment the 91st forged cordial relations with the French marine infantry which also formed part of the garrison, but within the regiment there had been considerable bad feeling between the commanding officer, Lieutenant-Colonel Glencairn Campbell, and Major Bertie Gordon, his second-in-command. At one stage the latter was ordered home on leave due to what Lieutenant Dunn-Pattison's history calls 'intense friction'. From Gordon's papers it is clear that not only was he a combative individual but he expected high standards of himself and others.

By then the 91st was on the move again, this time to India. Its journey took it first to Egypt for the overland trip from Alexandria to Suez on the Red Sea (the canal had not yet been constructed). At the time, Egypt was ruled by a viceroy under the suzerainty of the Ottoman empire and the holder of the post, Khedive Said Pasha, favoured France – he had granted Ferdinand de Lesseps the concession for constructing the Suez Canal – and was therefore wary of British interests in the area. For its part, Britain was alarmed by the French initiative – as the Foreign Office saw it, Bombay would soon be 4,600 miles from Marseilles and India's integrity could no longer be guaranteed. As a result of those tensions the 91st had to pass through Egypt as civilians, and without wearing their uniforms the men were transported by teams of donkeys to the port of Suez. The regimental digest described the scene:

> Here [the rail head] donkeys were in readiness to convey the troops across the seventeen miles of desert to Suez. They had been drawn up, as arranged by the Headquarter Staff, in sections of 30 rank entire. As each section was mounted it was caused to move off. Leaving an interval of about 30 yards between sections, and a further interval between companies of 100 yards. In this order the march proceeded at a steady pace of about four miles an hour, halting twice at the post stations. The sick were conveyed in passengers' vans, four of which followed the column, one carrying a small medicine chest and a skin of water.

IMPERIAL SOLDIERING

On arrival in India the regiment moved to Kamtee near Nagpur in the Central Provinces (today Madhya Pradesh). At the same time, Colonel Campbell was promoted to command a brigade in Burma and Bertie Gordon succeeded him as commanding officer. Every ounce of his enthusiasm and determination would be needed because the 91st had arrived at a place which Gordon described as 'the most barbarous, the most inaccessible, the most neglected, and the most forgotten station in British India'. Although the living conditions were indeed disgraceful, the posting allowed the regiment to take part in the final operations in the suppression of the Indian Mutiny under the operational command of Major-General Sir Hugh Rose (later Lord Strathnairn), a distinguished soldier and diplomat who had started his military career as an ensign in the 93rd Highlanders. A veteran of the war in the Crimea, where he acted as the senior liaison officer with the French forces, Rose had arrived in India in September 1857 and was placed in command of the forces in Central India. By then the mutiny was in its last stages and these were played out by a colourful cast of personalities who included Lakshmi Bai, the Rani of Jhansi, a Maratha princess who had been forced to give up her state by the East India Company, and Tatya Tope, who was still at large in Central India. By the time the 91st arrived both had been killed – the Rani in battle near Morar and Tatya Topi by hanging at Sipri – but there were still mopping-up operations to be completed and the regiment found itself undertaking 'several long and trying marches, without however being engaged with the enemy'.

The mutiny changed the way in which India was administered. On 1 November 1858 the authority for ruling the country was passed from the East India Company to the Crown, which was represented by the person of a Viceroy (Earl Canning) who would rule through a Supreme Council. Accompanying the announcement was the proclamation of an amnesty for those rebels who were prepared to lay down their arms and return to their homes, the only exceptions being those who had 'taken part in the murder of British subjects' or those who had been 'leaders or instigators in revolt'. As a result many surrendered, but those who had nothing to lose tended to hold out to the bitter end. Curiously, two of them were apprehended by the 93rd Highlanders shortly before the regiment left India. One was Sarvur Khan, who had been responsible for killing 73 women and 124 children at Cawnpore; the other was Mohamed Ali Khan, a Rohilkhand nobleman who had regarded the mutiny as a struggle for Indian independence. Both were hanged, but before the sentence was carried out they were well treated by Sergeant William Forbes-Mitchell, who put a stop to an attempt to force-feed the condemned men with pork. He also provided them with a last hookah and in his memoirs remembered Sarvur Khan, the son of a Pathan prostitute and an unknown British soldier, as a 'very good looking, light-coloured native in the prime of his life'.

On 8 July 1859 the mutiny was declared officially to be at an end and the 91st stayed on in the country for another nine years, returning to Britain in 1868 following their last tour of duty in Jubbulpore (Jabalpur), the capital of the Saugor and Nerbudda territories. During this period many of the reforms instituted in the wake of the Crimean War began to come into effect, but the main driver of change within the regiment was the commanding officer. A reformer by instinct and a man of considerable energy and resolution, Gordon set about improving the lot of the ordinary soldiers and their families by instituting a number of much-needed improvements at Kamtee. The living quarters were upgraded and a gymnasium was built, as well as a modern and well-equipped 'Soldiers' Coffee Room, Reading Room and Shop'. Gardens were created for growing flowers and cultivating vegetables and 'manly sports and recreations' were encouraged. At the same time, Gordon was instrumental in introducing a system of competitive educational tests which were used in addition to seniority to determine promotions in the non-commissioned ranks. Future generations also had cause to be grateful to Gordon, as under his direction the regimental records were preserved and put in good order with years of poor grammar and indifferent spelling being corrected. In a letter to Lady Hatherton 'commenting on Miss [Florence] Nightingale's strictures on the interior economy of British regiments in India' dated 7 November 1863, Gordon elaborated his thinking:

> My soldiers' gardens were a fair sight by day; but a still prettier one once a-week at night. Every Thursday, public orders notified the day before that 'The soldiers' gardens would be open for music and recreation at 6 o'clock pm.' I had built a stand for the band, and one for the drummers and pipers. A nice shed under which a Restauration – Cigars, Coffee, Tea, Sodas, Lemonades, Oranges, Cakes etc. Also a spacious round Dancing Floor. Standard lamps on each side of the broad walks. Large numbers of soldiers and their wives and children, officers and their wives present. Glees and choruses sung after the band ceased playing. Dancing got up. The women never joined, but the men danced Quadrilles, Waltzes and Polkas to the music of a Quadrille band, and reels to that of the bagpipes. This weekly fete obtained the name of 'Colonel Gordon's Cremorne' [Cremorne Pleasure Gardens in Chelsea, London] . . .

As soon as the regiment arrived in India it revived its pipe band, the officers donating £86 for the purpose (£6,047 today). This was the beginning of a campaign to restore Highland status to the 91st, for although the regiment was dressed as an English line infantry regiment, it still clung on to its Scottish roots and considered itself to be in no small measure a Highland regiment. With the energetic Gordon in command, steps were taken to try to rectify that problem by increasing the number of Scots serving in the 91st. At first the portents were not good. In 1863 the regimental roll showed that the Scots were in a distinct minority: 501 English, 323 Irish and only 241 Scots. (These figures reflected the army's recruiting statistics between 1853 and 1860, when England supplied 151,942 recruits, Ireland 71,557 and Scotland 33,019.) However, while Gordon was on home leave that same year he approached the Duke of Argyll and confided his plans to increase the proportion of Scots by providing an incentive for them to join the regiment. If the 91st were recognisably Scottish in name and uniform, argued Gordon, it would be easier to appeal to native Scots to join it instead of other regiments. Although the request for the restoration of full Highland status was turned down by the War Office, in May 1864 Queen Victoria gave her permission for the regiment to be styled as the 91st Argyllshire Highlanders, with the proviso that it did not wear the kilt. This meant wearing trews, and the Army Order announcing the change was clear that the 91st should be:

> . . . clothed and equipped as a non-kilted Highland corps. Tunics, as worn in all Highland regiments, trews, of the Campbell tartan. Chaco [shako], blue cloth with diced band and black braid. Forage Cap, Kilmarnock, with diced band. The officers to wear plaids and claymores. The alteration of the dress to take place from April 1st, 1865. The white waistcoat with sleeves, as issued to the Highland regiments, will not be worn by the 91st Foot.

There was a hint of compromise in the arrangements. The changes allowed the regiment to resume its original territorial title and to be designated as Highlanders, but the officers and men were not allowed to wear the kilt. Instead the 91st became a hybrid, wearing a Highland tunic, tartan trews and the Kilmarnock forage cap, a broad, flat and somewhat ungainly bonnet with a red and white diced band. As for the tartan, Campbell had been prescribed by Queen Victoria's order and this was supported by the Duke of Argyll, it being his family's tartan. However Colonel Gordon was less certain as he felt that it was too similar to the Government or Black Watch tartan which was worn by the 42nd Royal Highlanders and the 93rd Highlanders. Instead he suggested the Campbell of Cawdor tartan, which has a red stripe, and after a good deal of argument and counter-argument this was eventually chosen as the regimental tartan. (At first the duke opposed it as he considered it to be too similar to the tartan of the Atholls, traditional foes of the Campbells.) At the same time, the pipe band was officially restored and a pipe-major was appointed.

Another opportunity to regain full Highland status arose in 1871 when the Marquis of Lorne, the Duke of Argyll's eldest son, married Princess Louise, the fourth daughter of Queen Victoria. The regiment was given the privilege of providing a guard of honour for the ceremony at St George's Chapel, Windsor and the pipes and drums also played. Shortly afterwards the queen asked if there might be some distinction she could confer upon the regiment for its services. The new commanding officer, Lieutenant-Colonel John Sprot, immediately suggested that the kilt should be readopted, but this request was vetoed by the War Office on the grounds of expense. Instead Queen Victoria consented to the regiment being styled as '91st Princess Louise's Argyllshire Highlanders'; it was also permitted to bear on its colours the Duke of Argyll's boar's head crest surmounted with the motto *Ne obliviscaris* (do not forget) with Princess Louise's coronet and cypher.

The next five years, 1874–79, were spent on garrison duty in Ireland. (Between 1868 and 1874 the stations had been Aldershot,

Fort George and Edinburgh.) Following the deployment in Ireland the regiment's next tour of duty took it back to southern Africa in February 1879, when it embarked on the steamship *Pretoria* bound for Durban. Once again the area was in a state of turmoil following the rapid economic expansion of Cape Colony in the previous decade – diamonds had been discovered in Griqualand and this had attracted fresh investment, a new wave of immigrants and a need to develop the infrastructure. As white expansionism increased there was also a need to maintain a passive black African population, but far from acquiescing, there were outbreaks of unrest amongst the native Griquas, the Xhosa and the Pedi and Basotho in Transvaal. These were put down by the superior firepower of the British garrison, but to the colonial administration the main threat seemed to come from King Cetshwayo (or Cetewayo) of the Zulu nation and war quickly became inevitable. In a cynical piece of political manoeuvring, Cetshwayo was provoked into attacking and destroying a column of 1,200 British troops and African auxiliaries at Isandlwana on 20 January 1879. Although the defeat seemed to be redeemed by the heroic stand of a small outpost at Rorke's Drift a few days later, the British were outraged by the setback and reinforcements were rushed out to South Africa. As the *Pretoria* left Southampton the cheering crowds shouted out to the men of the 91st: 'Avenge the 24th!' (Later The South Wales Borderers, whose men had been present at Isandlwana and Rorke's Drift.)

When the 91st arrived in South Africa the situation was still fluid and confused. Following his defeat at Isandlwana Lord Chelmsford had regrouped his forces in Natal, a smaller column under the command of Colonel C.K. Pearson was under siege in a mission station at Eshowe in southern Zululand while a mobile column commanded by Colonel Evelyn Wood VC was operating to the north. This latter force scored a spectacular, if one-sided, success at Khambula on 29 March when the superior firepower of Wood's column accounted for the deaths of 3,000 Zulus armed only with spears and ancient muskets. The British losses tell their own story: 18 killed and 57 wounded. Encouraged by the victory, Chelmsford decided to march quickly to relieve Pearson's force at Eshowe, splitting his force into two divisions which numbered 3,390 British soldiers and 2,280 African auxiliaries. The 91st served in the first division with 2nd Foot or the Buffs (The Queen's), 57th Foot (later 1st Middlesex Regiment), 3/60th Rifles (later The King's Royal Rifle Corps) and 99th Foot (later 2nd Wiltshire Regiment). To make up time the men carried the minimum equipment apart from 70 rounds of ammunition per man for their breech-loading Martini Henry rifles, which had been introduced in 1871 and had quickly proved to be real man-stoppers. Although the column was discommoded by heavy rain during the first day's march the men were ready for battle when the Zulus attacked them at Gingindlovu, where they had spent the night drawn up in a defensive square with a wagon laager. (In the Zulu language the name means 'the place of he who swallowed the elephant', but the soldiers quickly christened it 'gin, gin, I love you'.) The regimental records described the alignment of the forces and give a good idea of the way British soldiers prepared for action against an enemy whose tactics were defined by a headlong charge towards their positions:

> When morning broke it was found that the country was too heavy to move the wagons: the Zulus also were observed to be advancing in considerable numbers from the direction of a hill beyond the Inyezane. The camp, which was square in shape, having sides about 130 yards long, had its wagons in the centre; the 60th were in line on the front face, the 57th on the right, and the 91st on rear face, except two companies of the regiment, which, together with the Buffs and 99th detachment, held the left

face; two Gatlings and two nine-pounders were distributed
at the corners in charge of the Naval Brigade. Behind the
91st was a battalion of the Natal Native Contingent.

Once again it was less of a pitched battle and more of a turkey-
shoot as the Zulus ran forward in their traditional horn-shaped
attacking formation. Although they showed their usual courage in
rushing the British positions, bare chests and flimsy weapons were
no match for the disciplined firepower of the British infantry and
the heavier pounding from the accompanying Gatling guns. The
actual fighting lasted just under 90 minutes – the 91st on the left
reckoned that they were under attack for only 20 minutes – and
soon the Zulus were fleeing from the field pursued by mounted
infantrymen. It was a victory which allowed Eshowe to be relieved,
but as an anonymous colour-sergeant in the 91st described it in a
report in the *Illustrated London News*, there was nothing to take
any pride in the aftermath of the fighting: 'Our men stood it well.
Nothing in the world could stand our fire. Really the fight was
splendid in one way; yet very hard to see our fellow creatures
sent to eternity.' The 91st's losses were one soldier killed and nine
wounded. Ahead lay the invasion of Zululand, which was quickly
accomplished by Chelmsford's columns, but this was a war with
little honour, leaving an officer of the 91st, Lieutenant W.R.H.
Crauford, to complain that the Highlanders had 'done hardly
anything of fighting in the open'. Once hostilities ceased the
regiment returned to Durban, where the regiment next provided
companies for the garrisons on Mauritius and St Helena. For the
latter detachment the only excitements came in January 1880
when the former French Empress Eugenie arrived on the island to
visit the spot where Napoleon's body had been buried. (She was
on her way to retrieve the body of her son Louis Napoleon, the
Prince Imperial, who had been killed in an ambush while serving

on Lord Chelmsford's staff.) South Africa was to be the regiment's home until 1885, when it moved to Ceylon after further tours of duty in Natal and Zululand. By then (see below) it had changed its identity and had become the 1st battalion The Argyll and Sutherland Highlanders.

93RD HIGHLANDERS

Following its exertions during the suppression of the mutiny the 93rd was destined to stay in the sub-continent until 1871. The first station was at Sabathu, described as a 'Gurkha town', some 5,000 feet above sea-level and close to Simla, where the women and families rejoined the regiment. A year later the regiment moved to Rawalpindi in the Punjab, where its average strength remained at 1,025 and the records show that the only losses during the year (1860) were 17 deaths to illness and 49 men discharged. During the posting the welcome news was received on 6 July 1861 that Queen Victoria had authorised that the regiment 'should be designated, in addition to its numerical title, the "Sutherland Highlanders" by which name it been popularly known at [sic], and for some time after, the period of it being raised'. Inevitably there were also setbacks. In February 1862 the depot was raided and a number of weapons were stolen, the records somewhat ruefully making the point that the thieves were well prepared: 'with their perfectly naked bodies carefully oiled, [they] came armed with a large knife which they did not hesitate to use if discovered'. More serious was an outbreak of cholera in nearby Kohat which caused the deaths of four officers, 61 soldiers, 13 women and 15 children. As the regimental medical officer William Munro made clear in his memoirs, this was a testing time for the regiment:

> The conduct of the men during this long visitation of
> diseases was admirable. There was everything to depress

them. They had seen comrade after comrade taken by the pestilence. They were greatly weakened by continual fevers. Scarcely a man but felt the workings of the cholera poison in his system, its presence being indicated by constant nausea, giddiness, difficulty of breathing, and cramps in the legs or arms. Notwithstanding this, however, there was never any approach to panic, no murmuring or shrinking from duties the most trying and irksome. At one time the same soldiers would be on hospital fatigue almost every day, rubbing the cramped limbs of groaning and dying men. Yet they never complained, never held back in even a single instance so far as is known.

Matters did not improve until the end of the year, when the regiment moved out of the Peshawar Valley to Sialkot, which Munro welcomed as a station 'well suited to the European constitution'. On arrival the size of the regiment was affected by the retirement of time-expired men who returned to Britain, leaving it with a strength of three field officers, five captains, three ensigns, six staff, 30 sergeants, 25 corporals, 20 drummers and 497 privates. Later in the year (1863), the 93rd joined a force under the command of Brigadier-General Sir Neville Chamberlain to put down an uprising of 'Hindustani fanatics, who had been a source of trouble on the frontier since 1823'. While taking part in the fighting in the mountainous Ambeyla Pass the regiment was ordered to support the 71st Highland Light Infantry in an attack to retake a position known as the Craig picquet after it had been overwhelmed by tribesmen on 19 November. Despite having to clamber up this steep and rocky hill while coming under sustained fire, the men of the 71st and the 93rd pressed home their attack supported by an artillery barrage and flanking fire provided by 5th Gurkhas and 5th Punjab Infantry. The fighting continued for several hours before

Craig picquet was retaken; during the fighting the 71st lost six soldiers killed and 26 wounded, including its commanding officer, Lieutenant-Colonel Hope, but the losses in the 93rd were confined to one man wounded.

For its remaining years in India the regiment was based variously at Ferozepore, Peshawar, Gwalior, Jhansi and Poona. Although there were complaints that the long period of service had a deleterious effect on the men, with an outbreak of protests about drunkenness in 1868 (surprising because the 93rd was generally considered to be a sober regiment), the annual reports were generally favourable, and in an attempt to keep the men occupied the commanding officer instituted a reading room at Peshawar. Not surprisingly this won Munro's approval because as the regiment's medical officer he and his staff were on the receiving end of the results of any inebriation:

> It was supported by the voluntary subscriptions of the men, sometimes numbering 400, and superintended by the chaplain, the Revd. Hugh Drennan. Besides books, periodicals and newspapers, the men could play chess, backgammon, bagatelle and billiards. Large and comfortable, well warmed and lighted, and another room attached where coffee could be obtained, this place was a great addition to the comfort and enjoyment of the men, and it was also useful in lessening intemperance and crime. Other recreations such as quoits, football and cricket were provided, also a gymnasium where single stick and boxing were taught, and a dance club was formed.

The only problem with the last idea was one of interpretation: most soldiers favoured dancing Highland reels while a handful held out for 'the modern and foreign form of dance' and a balance had to be found. Other diversions included the creation of vegetable gardens and the establishment of a regimental school of the children. Each year, during the cool season in February, the regiment held Highland Games and throughout the period the officers enjoyed rough shooting and other field sports. When the deployment in India came to an end at the beginning of 1870 ten sergeants, five corporals and 102 soldiers volunteered to transfer to other regiments so that they could stay on in India. For the rest of the regiment ahead lay the long voyage back to Scotland on board the troopships *Himalaya* and *Jumna* which arrived at Burntisland on 27 March. Special trains then took the men and their families to Stirling and Perth. At the time of the return the commanding officer was Lieutenant-Colonel F.W. Traill Burroughs, who was nicknamed 'wee Frenchie' on account of his size – he stood less than five feet – and the fact that he had been educated in France. There is an attractive portrait of this period in the writings of William Forbes-Mitchell, who had served in India throughout the unrest and had an especial affection for his old regiment, not least because of its close links with the Church of Scotland:

> The 93rd was no ordinary regiment. They were the most Scotch of all the Highland regiments; in brief, they were a military parish, minister and elders complete. The elders were selected from among the men of all ranks – two sergeants, two corporals and two privates; and I believe it was the only regiment in the army which had a regular service of communion-plate; and in time of peace the Holy Communion, according to the Church of Scotland, was administered by the regimental chaplain twice a year.

On returning to Scotland the regiment made its way to Aberdeen, where the depot companies were based, and received a warm welcome from the local people as it marched through the city. As a result of the home posting the regiment was reduced in size to 33 officers, 49 sergeants, 40 corporals, 18 drummers, five pipers and 480 soldiers. Ahead lay postings in Edinburgh and Aldershot followed by a return to Ireland where the regiment was based at the Curragh outside Dublin. This was followed by a posting to Gibraltar from January 1879 to March 1881, when the regiment returned to Aldershot. During the decade the 93rd underwent a series of dramatic changes which affected every infantry regiment in the British Army – the Cardwell/Childers reforms which produced a regimental system which remained in place until equally far-reaching reforms were introduced in 2004.

Soldiers often say that there is no British Army; instead it is a collection of regiments. There is some truth to the assertion. From the outset when it came into being in 1660 following the restoration of King Charles II, the six standing regiments were known as the king's 'guards and garrisons', and over the years the system of organising the regiments has undergone constant change. In the beginning, line infantry regiments were known more usually by the name of the colonel which brought them into being; a few also had territorial titles and 78 regiments or corps had royal titles as a mark of long and distinguished service or to reward gallantry in the field. Over the years there were significant changes to the structure of the infantry regiments. In 1751 the names of colonels were removed and numbers introduced by a Royal Warrant which listed the regiments in order of precedence: first the Life Guards and the Royal Horse Guards; second the cavalry regiments; third the three regiments of Foot Guards; fourth the line infantry regiments numbers 1st to 49th; and finally the Royal Regiment of Artillery. In 1861 a new order of precedence was produced which was broadly similar, with the exception that the Royal Regiment of Artillery, followed by the Corps of Royal Engineers, was placed between the cavalry and the Foot Guards, and the line infantry regiments were numbered 1st to 109th, followed by The Prince Consort's Own Rifle Brigade, which was unnumbered.

The next seismic change came in 1881 with the implementation of a reformed structure which was based on the concept of localisation. For some time the War Office had toyed with the idea of introducing a territorial system by which every regiment would be linked to its own local recruiting area. The result was the creation of Sub-District Brigade Depots which paired 141 infantry battalions at 69 brigade depots. Under this scheme in 1873 the 91st was linked with 72nd Highlanders (later 1st Seaforth Highlanders) at No. 58 Brigade Depot at Stirling. At the same time the 93rd was linked with 92nd Highlanders (later 2nd Gordon Highlanders) at No. 56 Depot at Aberdeen. Both conjunctions made sense, as the former brought together two unkilted Highland regiments while the latter linked two kilted Highland regiments.

However, further change was in the air. At the time, all infantry regiments numbered 1st to 25th and the two Rifle Brigade regiments (60th and 95th) had multiple battalions, and plans were now prepared to provide all single-battalion regiments with two battalions through a process of amalgamation. Under a process begun in 1872 under the direction of the Secretary for War, Edward Cardwell, and finalised nine years later by his successor, Hugh Childers, the remaining single battalion regiments were linked with others of their kind to form new two-battalion regiments and provided with territorial designations. Each regiment would also have local militia and volunteer rifle battalions consisting of part-time soldiers, the predecessors of the later Territorial Army. Under this refinement the 91st and the 93rd were amalgamated to form a new two-battalion regiment to be known initially as 'Princess Louise's Sutherland and Argyll Highlanders'. Within a year this was changed to the more accurate and less cumbersome title 'Princess Louise's (Argyll and Sutherland Highlanders)'. Driving the Cardwell/Childers reforms was the theory that one battalion would serve at home while the other was stationed abroad and would receive drafts and reliefs from the home-based battalion to keep it up to strength. As a result of the localisation changes regimental numbers were dropped and territorial names were adopted throughout the army but, as happens in every period of reform, the changes outraged older soldiers, who deplored the loss of cherished numbers and the introduction of what they held to be undignified territorial names, some of which bore no relation to the new regiment's traditions and customs.

However, at the time the combination of the Argyll Highlanders and the Sutherland Highlanders was reasonably harmonious as it proved possible to incorporate each regiment's history and traditions into the new formation. For a long time though, the two battalions continued to use their older numbers within the regiment to distinguish their separate historic identities and it was not until after the Second World War, when a further change in 1948 saw them being amalgamated into a single battalion, that the regiment came to be known colloquially as 'the Argylls'. At the time of the first amalgamation much was made of the connection with the founding fathers of the two regiments, the Dukes of Argyll and Sutherland. The new regiment adopted the mottos of the two families: *Ne Obliviscaris* (Do not forget), the motto of the Duke of Argyll, and *Sans Peur* (Without fear), the motto of the Duke of Sutherland, and the new regimental badge, which was designed by Princess Louise herself, included the Clan Argyll's boar's head and the Clan Sutherland's wild cat. It also allowed the 91st to achieve its ambition of wearing the kilt once again: the slightly lighter shade of the 93rd's government tartan was adopted by the new regiment, as was the distinctive sporran with its six tassels. At the same time, the rifle volunteer corps within the regiment's district were combined and incorporated into the regimental family as 1st (Renfrewshire), 2nd (Renfrewshire), 3rd (Renfrewshire), 4th (Stirlingshire), 5th (Argyllshire) and 7th (Clackmannan and Kinross). These were the predecessors of the Territorial Force which came into being on 1 April 1908 to provide the army with a new system of part-time volunteer soldiers for home defence. Each infantry regiment received a number of Territorial battalions based largely on the older volunteer corps battalions. In its final form, The Argyll and Sutherland Highlanders had five Territorial Force battalions numbered 5th to 9th (see Chapter Six).

FIVE

Pathans and Boers

For the first years of the regiment's new life the 1st battalion was the overseas battalion while the 2nd battalion formed the home service battalion, sending regular drafts and reliefs to the former. For example, in 1892 when the 1st battalion returned to Scotland from tours in Ceylon and Hong Kong, 400 men transferred to the 2nd battalion in order to complete their period of service in India. However, although the system had been broadly welcomed by the army and in this instance served the new regiment well, it was still not altogether efficient. Throughout the remainder of the century most home-based battalions in the British Army experienced immense problems in finding the necessary numbers of men and were often so depleted that they had difficulty keeping up to strength themselves. All too often they had to enlist volunteers from other regiments or had to call on reservists to make up numbers. For the 2nd battalion this was a particular problem, as under the reforms it lost the counties of Caithness and Sutherland to the new Seaforth Highlanders (72nd and 78th); in return the two battalions of The Argyll and Sutherland Highlanders were expected to recruit from Argyllshire, Dumbarton, Renfrew, Stirling, Clackmannan and Kinross. Only one of these counties, Argyllshire, was wholly Highland, and as Brigadier Cavendish noted 'the 93rd, as time went on, became more Lowland, and with a larger proportion of English and Irish in its ranks'. At the same time the depot companies moved from Aberdeen to Stirling, which became the new regiment's headquarters.

Due to the slow pace of reform within the army, pay remained low and conditions continued to be antiquated, and as a result recruiting targets were rarely met. For example, a government report into the condition of barracks in 1859 described Stirling Castle as 'the worst barracks we have seen anywhere'. Marriage was still discouraged, drunkenness was often rife and those who left the army often became unemployed vagrants or burdens on society. With the steady decline of the rural population a traditional source of recruitment was drying up; this was a particular problem for regiments like the Argylls, whose recruitment hinterland was largely made up of country areas. Despite the abolition of purchasing commissions, the social background of the army's officers did not change and the regiment's officers still came from the aristocracy, the landed gentry, the clergy and the professions, and had been educated at one of Britain's great private schools. There were exceptions: as we have seen, William McBean VC of the 93rd was commissioned from the ranks and never lost his Scottish accent, and Surgeon Munro provided evidence that in the 91st and 93rd the gap between officers and men was not as wide as many might have believed to be the case in the Victorian army:

> There existed generally or almost universally, a friendly feeling which extended throughout all ranks, but I think that in Scotch or Highland Regiments there was something more than this. In these there was a friendly intimacy

between Officers and men, which by strangers might seem to have been looked upon as familiarity, but which was in reality the evidence of esteem and confidence in each other which knew no fear and was the result, not only of long companionship, but of a feeling of nationality.

In any case, it was not all stagnation and conformity: the same period saw a number of successful innovations. The earlier introduction of the new breech-loading rifles had helped to increase the rate and weight of fire and this was assisted by the use of new smokeless propellants. The Royal Artillery started receiving breech-loading ordnance and in the Maxim gun the army possessed a reliable automatic machine-gun which gave it the astonishing firepower of 2,000 rounds a minute. In Garnet Wolseley the army also produced one of the great military reformers of the late nineteenth century. One of the rising stars in the British Army, Wolseley's career mixed staff appointments with operational command of small imperial military expeditions and as he climbed up the army lists he made a point of personally selecting his officers and nurturing military talent. In time the officers who served with him would be known as the 'Wolseley Ring' and once they had come to his notice their careers usually prospered. A rival 'ring' was formed by Roberts in India, but Wolseley's was the more influential of the two. In 1869 he had published *The Soldier's Pocket Book* which became the standard military textbook of its day with its insistence on the need for thorough and painstaking preparation before undertaking any operation. Wolseley was also an experienced soldier: having served as a subaltern in Burma, China, India and the Crimea he had gone on to make his name as an operational commander in Canada (Red River Expedition, 1870) and the Ashanti War of 1873–74. Not for nothing was the phrase 'All Sir Garnet' a byword for efficiency and good practice. In 1895 he became commander-in-chief of the

British Army, succeeding his great rival, the deeply conservative Duke of Cambridge.

One thing neither Wolseley nor his army was ever denied – the chance to see operational service. Between 1883 and 1914 not a year passed without British soldiers being in action in one part of the empire or the other. Although the operations were usually policing actions against unequal native opposition they allowed the new weapons to be tested and, above all, they made soldiers familiar with battle-field conditions. Drawing from his own career, Wolseley argued that experiences of this kind were absolutely essential, especially 'the sensation of being under fire'. It helped too that the opposition was varied – tribal warriors with primitive weaponry but unlimited courage (Maoris, Ashanti, Zulus), hillmen with an intimate knowledge of the lie of the land (Afghans and Pathans), fundamentalists with no fear of death (Dervishes and Mahdists), well-organised infantry (Egyptians) and equally skilful mounted infantry (Boers). All those operations brought different challenges to the soldiers who experienced them and helped to fashion the late Victorian and Edwardian soldier in the three decades before the outbreak of the First World War.

1ST BATTALION ARGYLL AND SUTHERLAND HIGHLANDERS

The 1st battalion remained in South Africa until 1885, when it moved to Ceylon as part of the Indian garrison. With its absence of any internal tensions and possessed of some breathtaking scenery and an equable climate, the island provided a pleasant posting for the regiment. The records show that the officers and men were able to take full advantage of the sporting facilities available to them and to enjoy excursions further afield to Kandy, Newera Eliya and Trincomalee. Three years later this was followed by a first deployment to Hong Kong (1886–91). This vital port and trading centre had been in British hands since 1842, when it was ceded by the Treaty of Nanking as an open port and further territory was acquired on the mainland at Kowloon in 1860. At the end of the tour of duty the battalion returned to Scotland and was based firstly in Edinburgh and then in Glasgow. (At the time the main garrisons and barracks in Scotland were located at Inverness, Aberdeen, Dundee, Perth, Stirling, Edinburgh, Greenlaw, Hamilton, Ayr, Paisley, Glasgow, Dumbarton, Fort William and Fort Augustus.) In August 1899 the battalion was warned to prepare for war service in South Africa, where trouble had been fomenting with the Boers. Mobilisation began in October and 1st Argylls left for the war zone on board SS *Orcana*, arriving at Cape Town on 19 November.

Britain had been at loggerheads with the Boers – Dutch immigrants who had settled in Cape Colony – for most of the century. As we saw in the previous chapter, the Boers had trekked north to establish Transvaal and the Orange Free State, but that did not solve matters and the enmity broke out into open war in 1880 as a result of non-payment of taxes. Following the humiliating defeat of a British force at Majuba Hill an uneasy peace was restored, with the Boers operating self-government under British suzerainty, but it was a powder keg awaiting the spark. The fuse was provided in 1886 by the discovery of seemingly limitless supplies of gold in Boer territory south of Pretoria. The lure of untold riches attracted speculators from Britain and all over Europe and before long the Boers were outnumbered by outsiders who threatened their traditional conservative way of life. To protect his fellow Boers in the Transvaal, President Kruger passed stringent laws excluding non-Boers from participation in political life while retaining the right to tax them.

Such a state of affairs was bound to cause trouble, but when it came in 1895 it proved to be a botched business. Acting in the mistaken belief that an uprising against the Boers was imminent the British imperial adventurer Cecil Rhodes encouraged his associate, Dr Starr Jameson, to lead a raid into the Transvaal to bring down Kruger's government. It was an abject failure but the Jameson Raid had far-reaching consequences. Rhodes was disgraced and Britain was made a laughing stock, and to make matters worse the subsequent negotiations to retrieve the situation settled nothing. Each new concession was met with further demands and gradually war became inevitable. In 1899 Britain despatched 10,000 troops to South Africa to bolster its garrison while the Transvaal, now backed by the Orange Free State, made plans for mobilisation. War was declared on 12 October after Kruger's demands that Britain remove her troops from the frontier were ignored in London and within a week General Sir Redvers Buller VC was on his way to South Africa to take command of the imperial forces in what everyone hoped would be a short, sharp war.

Amongst the battalions serving under Buller was 1st Argylls, which had been assigned to the Highland Brigade together with 2nd Black Watch, 1st Highland Light Infantry (HLI) and 2nd Seaforth Highlanders. Commanded by Major-General Andrew Wauchope, an eminent Black Watch officer who had served in Egypt and Sudan, the Highland Brigade formed part of General Lord Methuen's 1st Division together with the Guards Brigade. However, when the Argylls and other reinforcements started arriving in South Africa the tactical situation was still fluid. The Boers had moved quickly to invest Mafeking and Kimberley, and to relieve both places Methuen had begun assembling a relief column on the Orange River with the intention of advancing along the Cape Town–Kimberley railway line. Shortly after arriving, 1st Argylls was detached to join this force, serving in 9 Brigade, and first saw action on 28 November at the point where the railway line crossed the Modder and Riet rivers.

In this initial stage of the battle the Boers held the advantage of concealed positions where they had positioned their artillery – 75-pounder Krupp field guns and one-pounder Maxims – and they made good use of them by ambushing Methuen's column. For ten hours under the blistering sun the Boers were able to pin down the advancing British infantry. As the war correspondent Arthur Conan Doyle described the situation, it was a grim foretaste of the kind of war the British Army would soon be fighting against an enemy who knew the lie of the land and understood how to use it:

> As the afternoon wore on a curious condition of things was established. The guns could not advance and would not retire. The infantry could not advance and would not retire. The Guards on the right were prevented from opening out on the flank and getting round the enemy's line, by the presence of the Riet River, which joins the Modder almost at a right angle. All day they lay under a blistering sun, the sleet of bullets whizzing over their heads . . . The men gossiped, smoked and many of them slept. They lay on the barrels of their rifles to keep them cool enough for use. Now and again there came the dull thud of a bullet which had found its mark, and a man gasped, or drummed with his feet; but the casualties at this point were not numerous, for there was some little cover, and the piping bullets passed for the most part overhead.

Eventually the stalemate was broken by 9 Brigade on the left where the river was crossed and the Boers began to retire as the British artillery began to get their range. In Conan Doyle's estimation 'the honours of the day upon the British rested with the Argyll and Sutherland Highlanders, the 2nd Coldstreams and the artillery', but it came at a price. Of the 468 casualties (killed and wounded) in

Methuen's force 112 came from the Argylls. After the battle, which Methuen counted as 'the hardest-won victory in our annals of war' – an exaggeration but he had good reason to feel relief at driving off the Boers – 1st Argylls rejoined the Highland Brigade for the next phase of the advance.

On the night of 10/11 December the brigade's task was to engage a new Boer position at Magersfontein Kopje, a rocky outcrop whose features reminded the advancing British soldiers of the prow of a battleship. The encounter on the River Modder had provided some indication of how the Boers would fight. Magersfontein would add to that lesson with interest, but from the very outset the operation was doomed. Not only was the reconnaissance of the Boer position sketchy and amateurish but the men of the Highland Brigade had to make a night march to get into position for a dawn attack, always a risky undertaking, and doubly so when the lie of the land is unknown. To complicate matters there was a torrential downpour during the night, leaving the men wet and cold as they did not carry greatcoats. Prior to the assault British artillery opened heavy fire on the Boer positions in the heaviest bombardment mounted by the British Army since the siege of Sevastopol over 40 years earlier. To the watching war correspondents it seemed that nothing could have survived such a barrage, but they were not to know that the Boers were not on the kopje but had taken up new positions in a long line of trenches which lay below it. Unfortunately, these remained undisturbed by the bombardment and this meant that when the Highland Brigade went into the attack they would be facing sustained and accurate rifle fire from the hidden Boers.

So it proved. At four o'clock in the morning the Highland Brigade column approached the Boer lines with A and B companies 2nd Black Watch in the lead, followed by 2nd Seaforth and 1st Argylls with 1st HLI in general reserve. As the battalions moved forward Wauchope gave the order to extend the line in preparation for the assault on the Boer positions. As he did so, a heavy fusillade broke out from the Boer trenches only 400 yards away and although much of the shooting was initially too high it caused momentary panic and disorder. Thinking to extend his line to the right to outflank the Boer trenches, Wauchope turned to his aide-de-camp (ADC) and cousin Lieutenant (later Major-General) A.G. Wauchope and told him to pass the order to the Seaforths and the Argylls to position themselves to the right of 2nd Black Watch. Although the ADC managed to give the order there was further confusion when the Argylls' commanding officer was killed and this was followed by the death of General Wauchope, shot down in the heavy rifle fire. 'The intensity of the fire seemed tremendous,' remembered an Argylls officer later. 'I can distinctly remember standing absolutely thunder-struck at what seemed like a shower of bullets whistling past on all sides.' As dawn broke the position of the Highland Brigade was hopeless. With their general dead the command structure had collapsed and the survivors were pinned down on the veldt under the hot sun and an easy prey to Boer snipers. A reminiscence by Colour-Sergeant McInnes, published in the 91st's regimental history, provides a telling account of the men's predicament:

> Immediately on the level in front of us, a concealed trench opened a terrific fire. The front of the hill was lit up by the flashes of rifles as though someone had pressed a button and turned on a million electric lights. The brigade seemed to stagger under the awful fire, but yet held their ground, and did not break. The order was given to lie down, but in that close formation we were getting shot like sheep. I remember distinctly the 91st getting the order to move to the right, and we had started to move in that direction

> when several very contradictory orders rang out, some
> calling to 'fix bayonets and charge' etc. . . . Then several
> started to shout 'retire', and the next minute the brigade
> lost all shape, and were converted into a dismayed mob,
> running to seek cover anywhere and getting shot by the
> score as they did so.

Amidst the carnage Piper James Mackay of 1st Argylls tried to rally the men by standing up and playing 'The Campbells are Coming' but his courage was to little avail. Nine hours later, without food or water and tormented by the scorching sun, which burned the back of the men's legs below their kilts, the nerve of the Highland Brigade broke. As they began a panic-stricken retreat to safety the Boer riflemen again took their pick of choice targets. The casualties reflected the scale of the disaster. The Highland Brigade lost 210 killed and 738 wounded; the casualties in 1st Argylls were three officers and 32 soldiers killed.

The news of the disaster caused a tremendous shock when it reached Scotland. Not only were the cream of the country's regiments involved in the debacle and the resulting casualties high, but the defeat came at a time when Britain's soldiers were supposed to be invincible. (A year earlier, in September 1898, a joint British–Egyptian–Sudanese army commanded by Lord Kitchener had crushed Mahdist fundamentalists at the Battle of Omdurman.) The misery was compounded by news of two other heavy defeats at Stormberg and Colenso, a period of setbacks that was promptly christened 'Black Week'. On the streets of Edinburgh women wept openly and social occasions were hurriedly cancelled; but there was a sense of shame, too, that such a distinguished brigade of Highland regiments should have been forced to retire from the battlefield in front of the rest of the British Army. 'Never has Scotland had a more grievous day than this of Magersfontein,' noted Conan Doyle.

'She has always given her best blood for the Empire, but it may be doubted if any single battle has ever put so many families of high and low into mourning from the Tweed to the Caithness shore.'

In an attempt to retrieve the situation in the wake of the disaster the troop levels in South Africa were increased, Buller was sacked and command of the army was given to Lord Roberts. His chief of staff and second-in-command was Kitchener, fresh from his exploits in Sudan. In the Highland Brigade Wauchope was replaced by Major-General Hector Macdonald, a remarkable Gordon Highlander who had risen from the ranks and was known throughout the army as 'Fighting Mac'. The changes lifted spirits and immediately brought results. The new year, 1900, began with the lifting of the siege of Kimberley and in February Kitchener smashed the Boers into submission at Paardeberg in a hard-pounding battle which lasted the better part of a week. During the fighting the four battalions of the Highland Brigade made a frontal attack on the Boer positions and once again they were pinned down by accurate rifle fire. This time they did not lose their heads but there were still casualties. Conan Doyle was amongst those who were impressed by the steadfastness of the Highland regiments:

> A great military authority has stated that it takes many years for a regiment to recover its spirit and steadiness if it has been heavily punished, and yet within two months of Magersfontein we find the indomitable Highlanders taking without flinching the very bloodiest share of this bloody day – and this after a march of thirty miles with no pause before going into action. A repulse it may have been, but they bear no name of which they may be more proud upon the victory scrolls of their colours. [Paardeberg is a regimental battle honour, see Appendix.]

During the fighting the 1st battalion lost 18 soldiers killed and five officers and 78 soldiers wounded. Also killed in the attack was Colonel Ormelie Campbell Hannay, a distinguished Argyll and former commanding officer of the 91st who was commanding the Mounted Infantry Brigade. (In common with every other regiment, the 1st battalion provided officers and men for the Mounted Infantry, a force of 20,000 troopers who acted as scouts and rapid response forces. The 91st Mounted Infantry Section served under the command of 2nd Lieutenant G. E. Courtenay in 2nd Mounted Infantry Battalion.) Paardeberg helped to break the back of Boer resistance and in its aftermath the Highland Brigade came out of the line and was employed on the demanding task of guarding the lines of communication.

This was the turn of the tide and the war entered a new phase with the invasion of the Orange Free State and the Transvaal. By September Pretoria and Johannesburg had been occupied, the Boer army under the commandant-general, Martinus Prinsloo, had capitulated at Brandwater Basin. During this period the Argylls served in the Orange Free State and saw action during the advance on Bloemfontein, the march to Heilbron and Koomati Poort and at Rustenburg between October 1900 and April 1901 when it provided outposts for local defences and guarding lines of communication. To all intents and purposes the war was over. The main Boer strongholds were in British possession, the lines of communication had been secured and the Boer leadership was fractured, but the fighting was destined to last another 18 months in its third and final phase. At the end of the year Roberts handed over command to Kitchener, but instead of tying up the loose ends the new commander-in-chief found himself engaged in a lengthy and bitter guerrilla war with an enemy who refused to give up the fight.

Before leaving South Africa Roberts described the Boers as 'a few marauding bands' but he had underestimated their strength and determination. In fact, some 30,000 Boer guerrillas were still in the field and they were determined to continue the fight. As long as they had rifles and ammunition and a sense of burning loyalty to the Boer cause they saw no reason to surrender, or as they put it to turn into 'hands-uppers'. As soldiers, they understood that the numerical superiority of the British Army made outright victory impossible, but they took heart from the sheer size of their country and the support they received from their kinsfolk. Most of the veldt was still free and the guerrillas made it their home, using deception, speed and marksmanship in place of fortification and artillery. The battalion came face to face with this type of warfare while serving with a column commanded by Colonel G.E. Benson, Royal Artillery, which also contained two battalions of mounted infantry and six field guns, as well as engineering and medical support. Its target was a group of Boer commando forces under the command of Assistant-Commandant-General Ben Viljoen which were roaming at will over the Eastern Transvaal. On 3 July 1901 Benson's Column surprised the Boers at Vlakfontein, killing six of them and capturing large numbers of horses and cattle. Against an enemy which *The Times History of the War* called 'shy and wild as grouse in December' the action was considered a singular success and a vindication of the use of mobile columns.

With his army stretched out along the main lines of communication, Kitchener decided to turn the position to his own advantage. He began by ordering a series of drives across the country to sweep the Boers out of their hiding places. Everything in the path of the advancing infantry had to be destroyed, with the result that the army found itself facing large marauding gangs of farmers, plus their women and children, swarming over the blackened remains of a ruined countryside. His solution to that problem was to house the dispossessed, and the families of Boers who had surrendered, in protected camps alongside the main railway lines until the hostilities came to an end. The camps were run on military lines and basic rations and accommodation were provided but the formation of these 'concentration camps' (as they were known) caused great outrage. Nonetheless, from a military point of view Kitchener's tactics did work. As a result of being housed in the camps the local population could not help the guerrillas in the field, and the sweeps and drives helped to round up large numbers of Boer fighters. The policy was helped by the construction of block-houses linked by wire fences which compartmentalised the countryside and removed the Boers' greatest assets – mobility and the ability to melt away into the hidden reaches of the veldt. It was a time-consuming exercise which tried the patience and endurance of the British Army, the regimental history noting tersely that 'some companies were engaged in the not very pleasant duty of removing Boer families from their farms'. For the 1st battalion that was its story for the rest of the war, which eventually drew to a close in the spring of 1902 and was concluded by the signing of the Treaty of Vereeniging.

When the 1st battalion left Ireland to join the army in South Africa in October 1899 it numbered 1,080 soldiers and during the course of the war it was reinforced by around 1,500 men from the 2nd battalion, the militia and new recruits. It was also reinforced by volunteer companies from the 3rd Militia Battalion which served at Bloemfontein (1st Volunteer Company), Middelburg (2nd Volunteer Company) and Eerste Fabrieken (3rd Volunteer Company). The 1st battalion remained in South Africa until the following year when it returned to Britain on board HMS *Syria* and spent most of the period based in the Aldershot area. In 1909 it moved to Malta (Imtarfa Barracks) prior to a posting to India, where it was based at Dinapore and Dum Dum in Bihar under the command of Lieutenant-Colonel H. L. Henderson.

2ND BATTALION ARGYLL AND SUTHERLAND HIGHLANDERS

As the home service battalion, 2nd Argylls remained in Britain until it moved to India at the end of 1891, arriving at Karachi before moving to its new stations at Dagshai and Ambala in the northern Punjab. Before leaving for the sub-continent the battalion attempted to rectify the difficulty of attracting new recruits by sending a detachment of recruiters into the western Highlands. This was done at the expense of the battalion's officers, but in spite of putting on a brave show the party failed to encourage a single recruit to take the Queen's Shilling. Shortly after arriving in India the battalion was re-equipped with the Lee Metford rifle, the first magazine weapon with a .303 calibre and a range of 600 yards (a spring inside the magazine forced the rounds up into the breech). As was the case with any regiment serving in India at that time, the records describe an easy-going existence with a timetable of military exercises interspersed by recreational activities with a great emphasis on sport. The only black cloud was an outbreak of fever in 1892 which left 14 men dead.

The bucolic atmosphere was interrupted in the following year by the battalion's involvement in one of the many wars which continually disrupted life on the North-West Frontier between India and Afghanistan. The reasons for the British presence in this remote and mountainous region had come about as a result of the annexation of the Punjab in 1848 and had then been exacerbated by Russia's territorial ambitions in Afghanistan as a means of threatening British rule in India. As a result the frontier became an important, if awkward, area which required constant policing, and that was never going to be an easy matter given the mettlesome independence displayed by the resident population. Seen on the map the frontier was defined by the River Indus and the plains and foothills which lay beyond it. And in the far distance towered the mountainous areas of the Hindu Kush which were populated by the warlike hill men of Waziristan. Not all of them were inclined to make trouble – the tribes in Baluchistan tended to be fairly pacific if left to their own devices – but it was a different matter dealing with the Pathan tribes in the area between Chitral and Baluchistan where the British had to maintain control of the strategically important Khyber, Kurram and Bolan mountain passes. It was an area which was to become familiar to countless British soldiers who quickly learned that their opponents were hardy hill men who, in the words of the poet Rudyard Kipling, did not give any mercy and did not expect to receive any:

> When you're wounded and left on Afghanistan's plains
> And the women come out to cut up what remains
> Just roll to your rifle and blow out your brains
> An' go to your Gawd like a soldier.

To meet the threat posed by the Pathan tribesmen the British Army evolved a policy which was known as 'butcher and bolt'. Basically this meant keeping its forces in the plains and only entering the mountainous tribal areas if there was trouble to be put down. When the tribes became too aggressive and started breaking the peace a punitive expedition would be mounted, the rebellious behaviour would be tamed by killing as many men as possible and then truces would be enforced which involved the surrender of weapons or the payment of a substantial fine. It was understood by both sides that no promises were binding and it was also recognised that violence would inevitably break out again after a suitable period of calm.

Later in the century the government in India attempted to develop a 'forward policy' of engagement with the tribal leaders to provide them with education and economic development in an attempt to break the cycle of violence. However, this was rarely successful because it was never developed wholeheartedly. Those in favour of the policy thought it ridiculous that large numbers of troops and resources should be tied down to solve a problem that was incapable of solution by force alone. Amongst the leading proponents was Lord Curzon, the forceful and energetic Viceroy of India at the beginning of the twentieth century, who claimed that the problem could be resolved by the imposition of law and order and the subsequent implementation of education, economic aid and a modern infrastructure. It was a laudable hope – the same problem continues to exist in the country in the twenty-first century – but within the Indian Army and the British regiments serving in India there remained a feeling that war on the frontier was good for training and building up morale. At the end of the nineteenth century hardly a year passed without punitive expeditions being mounted to punish recalcitrant tribesmen and names like Waziristan, Chitral, Tochi, Tirah and Malakand became part of the vocabulary of the British soldier.

The worst year was 1897 when a British political officer and his six-man escort were killed by Waziri tribesmen at Maizar in the Tochi Valley. This was followed by further outbreaks of unrest in the Swat Valley and Chitral all aimed at destabilising the region; as Winston Churchill, a young officer in the 4th Queen's Own Hussars, saw it, the frontier was suddenly ablaze and Britain's forward policy was in danger of falling apart:

> A single class had viewed with quick intelligence and intense hostility the approach of British power. The priesthood of the Afghan border instantly recognised the full meaning of the Chitral road. The cause of their antagonism is not hard to discern. Contact with civilisation assails the superstition, and credulity, on which the wealth

and influence of the Mullah depend. A vast but silent agitation was begun. Messengers passed to and fro among the tribes. Whispers of war, a holy war, were breathed to a race intensely passionate and fanatical. Vast and mysterious agencies, the force of which are incomprehensible to rational minds, were employed. The tribes were taught to expect prodigious events. A great day for their race and faith was at hand. Presently the moment would arrive. They must watch and be ready. The mountains became as full of explosives as a magazine.

As the unrest spread, Britain started taking measures to deal with it. Three field forces were raised to march into the mountainous border areas, one of which, the Tochi Valley Field Force contained 2nd Argylls which joined 1st Punjabs, 1st Sikhs and 35th Punjabs in 1 Brigade under the command of Brigadier-General Egerton. The brigade was supported by one squadron of the 1st Punjab Cavalry and a field company of the Bengal Sappers and Miners together with a battery of mountain guns. During the operation 2nd Argylls consisted of 22 officers, 778 soldiers reinforced by three officers from the Royal West Kents and two from The Buffs. Having assembled at the railhead at Nowshera the battalion advanced to Sharani before heading for Maizar which was promptly destroyed at the end of July. Rapid movements were hindered by the searing summer temperatures and later in the year by unseasonable rain. By October winter clothes were issued and in the following month the Waziri leader Sadda Khan entered into negotiations which brought the campaign to an end. For the battalion it had been an interesting if exasperating incident. It had given them experience of coming under fire and engaging a mobile enemy, but the operation had achieved little. Although the Waziri tribes agreed to pay the levied fines they remained hostile to the British, a fact acknowledged by Queen Victoria at the end of the campaign when she wrote to Viceroy Lord Elgin complaining that she could 'not help fearing that there was a want of preparation, of watchfulness, and of knowledge of what the wild tribes were planning, which ought not to have been'.

The battalion returned to the Punjab in January 1898 before transferring to less agreeable conditions in Central India, where the temperature rarely fell below 80 degrees Fahrenheit during the pre-monsoon season, and only dawn and dusk provided solace from the heat. The regimental records provide a graphic account of the conditions endured by the battalion during the hot season:

> Few can be seen out of their bungalows during the day, except those whose duty it is to draw the mid-day lotion from the canteen (this is done in cans provided for the purpose in which it is taken to the bungalow and issued to the thirsty individuals who possess the necessary), or the much abused punkah [fan] coolie who can be dimly seen under his straw shelter, giving the punkah lever the minimum of 'kinching' compatible with moving it at all. The sentries of the quarter guard are about the only other animate objects that can be seen, and they pass their two hours 'sentry go' as best they can under the meagre shelter afforded by the verandah, scorched with the hot air, that almost furnace heat that comes over the maidan [square] in front of the guardroom and blinking at the glare outside and the hot vapour that dances in seemingly endless eddies before their eyes.

While stationed at Miranshah 41 men succumbed to fever. In 1901 the battalion moved to Bengal and two years later there was another move, this time to the more welcome surroundings of the hill station at Poona, which was to be the 2nd battalion's final posting in India. In 1907 it moved to South Africa, travelling on board the troopship *Soudan* for a tour of duty at Bloemfontein. On leaving India the battalion numbered 18 officers, two warrant officers, 41 sergeants, 37 corporals, 21 pipers and drummers, 654 soldiers. By then the Lee Metford rifle had given way to the more robust Lee Enfield.

At the end of 1909 the battalion moved back to Britain and arrived at Maryhill Barracks on 28 January 1910 in driving snow, a stark contrast to the conditions they had endured during two decades of continuous overseas service. On Balaklava Day later in the year a dinner was held in Glasgow to commemorate the 93rd's part in the battle and 27 veterans attended it as guests of the battalion. In 1912 the 2nd Argylls moved again, this time north to Fort George under the command of Lieutenant-Colonel H.P. Moulton-Barrett.

SIX

The First World War: 1914–16

Many years later, long after the First World War had dissolved into memory, the summer of 1914 was remembered for its glorious weather and for the fact that it was the last period of peace before the world was plunged into over four years of hellish warfare. Only for those who cared to watch the distant horizon were there clouds of a different kind ready to spoil that high summer contentment. On 28 June came news that the heir to the throne of the Austro-Hungarian empire, Archduke Franz Ferdinand had been shot to death with his wife in Sarajevo, the capital of the province of Bosnia-Herzegovina. Initially the incident seemed to be an isolated terrorist attack and the first reaction was that the perpetrators would be caught and punished by the imperial authorities. At that stage there was no cause to believe that the assassination would plunge Europe into a global conflict. Even when it was reported that the blame for the outrage was being shifted on to neighbouring Serbia, the first of the Slav states to gain independence and a source of constant irritation in Vienna, there was no reason to believe that the task of hunting down those responsible would precipitate a crisis. At the time that the crisis was developing, in the middle of July, 6th Argylls, a Renfrewshire Territorial battalion, was enjoying its annual summer camp at Machrihanish in the Mull of Kintyre, where Major J.C. Barr remembered that there was golf and riding for the officers and everything seemed to be cosily familiar:

> The camp was similar in most ways to the training camps which some of us had attended for almost twenty years of service. The same canvas city gleaming white in the last rays of the setting sun, the same military routine, the same cheery mess tents and the same holiday spirit and jolly comradeship of old friends.

But even in that bucolic setting the war clouds were on the horizon. As the officers relaxed in the evening one of their number astonished the rest of the mess by reading aloud a newspaper report about 'trouble in the Near East' and musing that their battalion could soon be at its war station at Auchterarder in Perthshire. Those listening gave him short shrift: 'This remark was greeted with a round of incredulous laughter,' recalled Barr in his memoirs, 'but he only miscalculated the date by about a week.' The general opinion was that even if there was a war it would only be a local affair involving the two countries.

It was not to be: when it became clear that neighbouring Serbia might have been implicated in the attack the crisis deepened. On 23 July, weeks after the assassination, Austria–Hungary issued an ultimatum to Serbia, making ten demands for the suppression of Serb nationalist groups, the punishment of the assassins and participation in the judicial process. Serbia was given 48 hours to comply, and although the response was placatory its government stopped short of allowing Austria–Hungary to take part in the trial of the assassins, arguing that the matter should be referred to the

International Court at The Hague. That readiness to cooperate seemed sufficient to settle the matter, but already diplomacy was proving powerless to stop Europe's drift towards war. Both countries mobilised their armed forces when Germany, Austria–Hungary's main ally, encouraged Vienna to take decisive action against the Serbs before any other country intervened in the crisis. Confident of German support, on 28 July, Austria–Hungary declared war on Serbia, thus paving the way for a wider conflict. The following day, Russia, Serbia's traditional friend and protector, began to deploy its forces along the border with Austria and within 24 hours this was followed by the order for full mobilisation.

Although the move was made to discourage Austria it threatened Germany, which immediately demanded that Russia 'cease every war measure against us and Austria-Hungary'. On 1 August Germany declared war on Russia, followed two days later by a further declaration of war against France, Russia's ally. That same day German forces began crossing into Belgium as part of the pre-arranged Schlieffen Plan, to bypass the heavily fortified French frontier and encircle Paris from the north through Belgium. Britain, which had wanted to remain aloof from the crisis and was not formally in alliance with any of the main participants, was now about to be pressed into the conflict through a treaty of 1839 which guaranteed Belgium's neutrality. On 4 August, no answer having been received to an ultimatum that Belgium should remain unmolested, Britain declared war on Germany.

To meet the threat Britain's armed forces put into action previously agreed plans. At the end of its summer manoeuvres on 29 July the Royal Navy's Grand Fleet was ordered to sail from Portland through the Dover Straits north to its war station at Scapa Flow in the Orkney islands, where it was put on a war footing. The army, too, was on the move. As part of the 'Precautionary Period' of the Defence Plan Prior to Mobilisation, formations of the regular army based in Britain were told to return to their depots on 29 July. Most were on their annual summer camps or undergoing live firing exercises. The battalions of the Territorial Force were also mobilised and within a few days were given the opportunity of volunteering to serve overseas instead of remaining at their depots for home defence. Most agreed, including the regiment's four Territorial battalions. Plans were also laid to expand the size of the army. On being appointed Secretary of State for War, Field Marshal Lord Kitchener astonished his colleagues by stating that the war would last at least three years and it would require over a million men to fill it. On 8 August the call went out for the first 100,000 volunteers who would man the New Army (also known as Kitchener's Army) special service battalions. No new formations would be raised, but the existing infantry regiments would expand their numbers of battalions to meet the demand for men who would serve for the duration of the hostilities. By the war's end The Argyll and Sutherland Highlanders consisted of the following battalions:

1st Battalion (Regular Army) Dinapore, India, served with 81 Brigade, 27th Division

2nd Battalion (Regular Army), Fort George, served with 19 Brigade, variously in 6th Division, 27th Division, 2nd Division and 33rd Division (latterly in 98 Brigade)

3rd (Reserve) Battalion (Regular Army), Stirling

4th (Extra Reserve) Battalion (Regular Army), Paisley

1/5th (Renfrewshire) Battalion (Territorial Force), Greenock, served with 157 Brigade, 52nd (Lowland) Division and latterly with 34th Division

2/5th (Renfrewshire) Battalion (Territorial Force), Greenock

3/5th (Renfrewshire) Battalion (Territorial Force), Greenock

1/6th (Renfrewshire) Battalion (Territorial Force), Paisley, served as Pioneer Battalion, 5th Division and latterly, October 1918, with 51st (Highland) Division

2/6th (Renfrewshire) Battalion (Territorial Force), Paisley

3/6th (Renfrewshire) Battalion (Territorial Force), Paisley

1/7th Battalion (Territorial Force), Stirling, served with 10 Brigade, 4th Division and latterly, June 1916, with 51st (Highland) Division

2/7th Battalion (Territorial Force), Stirling

3/7th Battalion (Territorial Force), Stirling

1/8th (Argyllshire) Battalion (Territorial Force), Dunoon, served with 152 Brigade, 51st (Highland) Division and latterly, February 1918, with 61st Division

2/8th (Argyllshire) Battalion (Territorial Force), Dunoon

3/8th (Argyllshire) Battalion (Territorial Force), Dunoon

1/9th ((Dumbartonshire) Battalion (Territorial Force), Dumbarton, served with 81 Brigade, 27th Division and 10 Brigade, 4th Division

2/9th (Dumbartonshire) Battalion (Territorial Force), Dumbarton

3/9th (Dumbartonshire) Battalion (Territorial Force), Dumbarton

10th (Service) Battalion (New Army), Stirling, served with 27 Brigade, 9th (Scottish) Division and with 92 Brigade, 32nd Division

11th (Service) Battalion (New Army), Stirling, served with 45 Brigade, 15th (Scottish) Division and with 118 Brigade, 39th Division

12th (Service) Battalion (New Army), Stirling, served with
   77 Brigade, 26th Division

13th (Reserve) Battalion (New Army), Blackheath, served
   with 106 Brigade, 35th Division

14th (Service) Battalion (New Army), Stirling, served with
   118 Brigade, 39th Division; 120 Brigade, 40th Division
   and 42 Brigade, 14th Division

15th (Reserve) Battalion (New Army), Gailes, Irvine

16th Battalion (Territorial Force), formed from 3rd
   Provisional Battalion (Territorial Force), Sandwich,
   served with 221 Brigade

17th (Service) Battalion (New Army), Deal, absorbed with
   14th Battalion

At the outbreak of war the 1st battalion was serving in India and did not arrive back in England until November when, shortly afterwards, it crossed over to France to join 27th Division. By then the 2nd battalion had already been in action, as had 1/7th Argylls, the first of the regiment's Territorial brigades to reach the Western Front as part of 4th Division. Soon, every battalion in the regimental family would be at war, thus fulfilling that prophetic remark made in the evening sunshine at Machrihanish a few months earlier.

WESTERN FRONT
1st, 2nd, 1/6th, 1/7th, 1/8th, 1/9th, 10th, 11th, 12th and 14th battalions

At the outset of hostilities 2nd Argylls was based at Fort George and like every other regular infantry battalion in the British Army it had to be brought up to war strength by recalling its reservists. Being an unattached battalion with no brigade structure, 2nd Argylls was entrusted with guarding the British Expeditionary Force's

(BEF's) lines of communication, a task it shared with three other regular regiments, 2nd Royal Welch Fusiliers, 1st Cameronians and 1st Middlesex. However, within a short time of crossing over to France from Southampton the four battalions were placed in 19 Brigade and remained under force command. This meant that the brigade commander, Major-General L.G. Drummond, reported directly to the BEF commander, Field Marshal Sir John French, and not to II Corps commander, General Sir Horace Smith-Dorrien. The brigade was also tasked with providing a link to the French 84th Territorial Division as II Corps began digging into defensive positions along the Mons canal during the third week of August. This disposition was part of a pre-arranged plan for the BEF to move north to protect the left flank of the French line. While this was happening the French Fifth Army on the right had begun to withdraw following a heavy German attack on the Sambre. Poor intelligence on both sides meant that the senior commanders had little accurate information about what was happening along the Belgian border.

Although 2nd Argylls did not take part in the first engagement at Mons on 23 August, it did play a major role at the subsequent and more serious battle at Le Cateau a few days later, when II Corps turned to face the advancing Germans some 30 miles from Mons. It was the British Army's biggest set-piece battle since Waterloo and their 55,000 soldiers faced German opposition, which numbered 140,000. During the final stages of the fighting German buglers sounded the British 'Ceasefire' and officers were seen in front of the Argylls and 2nd Suffolks waving at the British to surrender. Nothing daunted, the Highlanders opened fire with deadly effect: two of their officers (Captains Maclean and Bruce) called out the hits as if they were at a shooting competition and not taking part in a fight for their lives. The British battalions were able to hold the line by dint of their superior firepower but by evening they were outnumbered and only a German failure to press home their advantage allowed them to resume their retreat. Even so, the casualties were heavy – 7,812 killed – and gave a stark indication of worse things to come. The casualties in the 2nd battalion were 160 killed or wounded and 300 missing. Exhausted by the battle and the summer heat, the BEF continued to pull back amidst rumours that the war was lost and that the French government had evacuated Paris for Bordeaux. It was a time of confusion, when the fog of war seemed very real indeed as the battle-weary infantrymen continued to sleep-walk – as it seemed – through the French countryside.

The Argylls were in reserve for the next phases of the fighting, the battles of the Marne and the Aisne, but the 2nd battalion was in the line near Armentières in support of the French during the First Battle of Ypres, which opened on 2 October. Although the bulk of the fighting took place north of the salient the battalion lost heavily. C Company almost ceased to exist and a battalion attack on the German lines on 9 November resulted in 130 casualties. By then the 1st battalion had arrived under the command of Lieutenant-Colonel H.L. Henderson, as had two Territorial battalions (1/7th in December 1914 and 1/9th in February 1915). All four battalions took part in the Second Battle of Ypres, which began on 22 April. The 1st battalion occupied a defensive position near Polygon Wood to the east of Ypres, with 1/9th Argylls in reserve. During the fighting the Germans used poison gas for the first time, although the initial attack achieved little due to adverse wind conditions. By the end of the month heavy German shelling obliged the division to realign its positions in Sanctuary Wood, a move viewed with misgivings as it brought 'our cordon round Ypres uncomfortably close to the city' (War Diary). During the battle the 1st battalion spent 36 days in the front line under more or less constant fire and as a result the casualties were high: three officers killed, 14 wounded or evacuated sick, 90 soldiers killed, 42 died of wounds and 339 wounded. On 19 May the battalion marched to bivouac in the area north of Vlamertinghe. The following week the battalion marched to Armentières headed by the pipes of the 10th battalion – 1st Argylls had lost its drums during the earlier Mons retreat – and on arrival at the new destination it was greeted by the pipes and drums of the 2nd battalion. It was the first time since 1873 that the two battalions had met while on the line of march. A different fate awaited the 1/9th battalion, which had been practically wiped out in the fighting on 17–18 May and was forced into a temporary amalgamation with 1/7th Argylls to form a composite battalion.

The major event of 1915 was the regiment's participation in the Battle of Loos in September, when half of the 72 battalions used in the assault phase bore Scottish titles. The battle also saw the blooding of Kitchener's New Army battalions: the 10th battalion served in 9th (Scottish) Division while the 11th battalion served in 15th (Scottish Division). Also taking part in the battle was the 2nd battalion, which went into action on the left of 19 Brigade and lost 315 killed and wounded in the opening minutes of the battle, largely as a result of lack of machine-gun support. The battalion's A Company lost all of its officers 'as soon as it moved' and the War Diary also shows that only 11 men from the two leading platoons succeeded in making their way back to the British trench lines.

Loos has been called many things by the soldiers who fought in it, and also by historians who have picked over its bones, but most are agreed that the best description is that it was both an unnecessary and an unwanted battle. In strategic terms it was meaningless. The attacking divisions gained a salient two miles deep and in the early stages of the battle some Scottish battalions had the heady sensation of advancing steadily across no man's land, but the end result did little to help a French offensive in Artois and Champagne, the main reason why Kitchener insisted that the battle should take place. At the same time, the Germans had learned the lessons of the Allied attacks earlier in the year and had created second defensive lines on the reverse slopes to compensate for their lack of reserves, and by occupying the higher ground they enjoyed an open field of fire. Both were used to good effect when the Allied offensive opened on 25 September and the high casualty figures tell their own story. Given the number of Scottish regiments involved in the battle, scarcely any part of the country was unaffected. The Argylls were no exception: in four days of fighting the 10th battalion lost 45 killed, 328 wounded and 116 missing, most of the latter almost certainly killed. The words of a poem written by Captain John Hay Beith, 10th Argylls (see Chapter Seven), had been written when the battalion moved across to France, but after Loos they had taken on a terrible new meaning:

> And now today has come along,
> With rifle, haversack and pack,
> We're off a Hundred Thousand strong,
> And – some of us will not come back.
> But all we ask, if that befall,
> Is this. Within our hearts be writ,
> This single-lined memorial:
> He did his duty and his bit.

As a result of the failings at Loos Sir John French was sacked as the BEF's commander-in-chief and replaced by General Sir Douglas Haig, the son of a whisky distiller with long-established roots in the Scottish Borders. His military philosophy and approach to the strategic situation on the Western Front were clear-cut. Looking at the trench system which separated the rival armies he argued that far from being permanent or an insuperable obstacle, it was the key to victory. Once the Allies had built up large enough armies backed by overwhelming firepower, they could attack and destroy the German positions with complete confidence. Successful infantry and artillery assaults would then allow cavalry to exploit the breakthrough by sweeping into open country to turn the German system of defence and ultimately defeat the enemy by removing its ability to resist. It was against that background that Haig contemplated the planning for the major offensive battle of 1916 – the Somme, which opened on 1 July and finally stuttered to a fitful conclusion in the middle of November. Three Scottish divisions were involved at the Somme – 9th and 15th Scottish Divisions (containing respectively 10th and 11th Argylls) and the 51st Highland Division (containing 1/7th and 1/8th Argylls) – but there were, of course, Argyll battalions serving in other divisions which also took part in the battle. But for a new deployment to the Salonika front (see below) the 1st battalion would also have taken part in the fighting on the Somme – it left France at the end of November 1915 having lost seven officers killed and 11 wounded, 129 soldiers killed, 61 died of wounds and 494 wounded.

During the initial stages of the battle in July, the 2nd battalion attacked German positions in the High Wood sector but the German lines proved to be difficult objectives and showed the limitations of the earlier British artillery bombardment. Similar problems faced the 1/7th battalion when the 51st (Highland) Division first went into the attack on 23 July, where the men found that they were being forced to cross a landscape littered with 'shell-holes, brambles, dense undergrowth and wire entanglements'. A week later the attack of the 1/8th battalion was countered by German artillery and the use of gas shells. In order to lull the Germans into a false sense of security there had been no preliminary bombardment and the assault battalions attacked in bright summer sunshine, with the result that casualties were high as the Highland Division moved forward towards the heavily defended German positions in the area beyond Fricourt towards Bazentin-Le-Petit Wood. During the fighting in July the losses in the 2nd battalion were 25 officers and 650 other ranks killed, wounded or missing while in one day (14 July) at Longueval the 10th battalion's losses were nine officers killed and ten wounded and 50 other ranks killed and 366 wounded or missing. When the 1/8th battalion made its attack on 27 July the losses were 80 dead and wounded. It was not until the first week of August that the bulk of the High Wood position fell into British hands.

By then 11th Argylls had joined the battle as part of 15th (Scottish) Division which attacked towards Martinpuich and its heavily fortified defences in mid-August. The same ground was attacked a month later in a new offensive along a 12-mile front south-west of Bapaume, and this proved to be the first time that tanks were used in the assault on the German positions. Towards the end of the battle the 14th battalion arrived in France but was not seriously involved in any of the combat operations. Its turn would come later. For the 1/6th battalion there was the unusual experience of transferring from the 51st (Highland) Division to serve in the 5th Division as a pioneer battalion, responsible for such essential tasks as building tracks and entrenchments and ensuring the mobility of the division. As a Renfrewshire battalion most of the men came from Paisley and there had been a keen sense of competition with the 1/8th battalion which, representing Argyllshire, regarded itself as a Highland formation. Many of its men were Gaelic speakers. Sometimes the rivalry got out of hand and led to fist-fights in the local estaminets. Much of the animus was created by the fact that 1/6th Argylls received weekly gifts of superior cigarettes presented by Bell's, a Paisley company, and were also given comforts by J.&P. Coates, the Paisley cotton manufacturers.

Given the substantial Scottish contribution to the Battle of the Somme, it was fitting that the last moves involved a large number of

Duncan Campbell of Lochnell, who raised the 98th (later 91st) Highlanders on behalf of his kinsman John, Duke of Argyll.

Major-General William Wemyss of Wemyss, who raised the 93rd Highlanders on behalf of the Countess of Sutherland in 1799.

Soldiers of the 91st engaging Hottentot warriors during the fighting in South Africa in 1850. Note the absence of tartan.

The 93rd Highlanders move into the attack during the Highland Brigade's assault on the Russian lines at the Battle of the Alma, 20 September 1854

A group of officers of the 91st at rest during the fighting in Zululand in 1879. Trews in Campbell of Cawdor tartan have been adopted.

The 2nd battalion on operations in the Tochi Valley on India's North-West Frontier in 1897. During the day temperatures reached 120 degrees.

Pipes and drums of the 1st battalion on the march in South Africa during the Boer War. A slouch hat gave some protection from the sun and a kilt apron covered the sporran.

Soldiers of the 2nd battalion at the beginning of the First World War. They are displaying a variety of weapons and an accordion presumably for off-duty relaxation.

Piper Murray of the 5th battalion in the trenches at Helles during the ill-fated Gallipoli campaign. He is wearing a brattie, or kilt apron, over his kilt.

Men of the 12th battalion on the march during the campaign in
Salonika in 1916. The 1st battalion served on the same front.

Highland dancers of the 1st battalion
being put through their paces at
Tidworth, 1937.

Jungle training in Malaya: the 2nd
battalion put a huge effort into
becoming proficient jungle fighters
and it paid off in the fighting against
the Japanese army in 1941–42.

An army marches on its stomach. Men of the 7th battalion
brew up during the fighting in Europe, 1944.

The long trail a-winding: the 8th battalion move up to the attack against
the enemy at Centuripe during the fighting in Sicily, 1943

Evacuation of casualties off Hill 282 during the Korean War. The wounded man is Lieutenant Jock Edington. Earlier the 1st battalion had been hit by a US 'friendly fire' air strike.

The use of helicopters proved to be essential during operations against Indonesian insurgents in Borneo. The 1st battalion carried out three operational tours in 1964 and 1965.

A dramatic painting by Peter Archer showing the moment when the 1ˢᵗ battalion began the operation to re-take the Crater district of Aden on 3 July 1967. Lieutenant-Colonel Colin Mitchell stands by the command vehicle accompanied by the adjutant Captain David Thomson.

On overseas operations British soldiers have always had a soft spot for the local children. It was no different when the 1ˢᵗ battalion served in Iraq in 2004 in the wake of the US-led operations to depose President Saddam Hussein.

Scottish formations including the 51st (Highland) Division, which was finally able to put behind it the setbacks encountered at High Wood. Not that the task facing the assaulting forces was any easier: following a dreadful late summer the weather deteriorated again in the autumn, making the ground conditions so bad that, according to the regimental historian of the 1/7th battalion, men were lost not just to bullets or explosives but also to the mud:

> There was no trench from Battalion Headquarters to the front line. There had been one, but it was no longer decipherable in the mud. Lengths of ship's rope were laid along the surface of the ground and fastened to iron pickets. Men had to grasp the rope, struggle on waist deep and keep their heads down, for even so much of them as was visible could be clearly seen by a number of active snipers. The front line itself, consisting of detached posts, was more or less a straggling pool of soft mud, and thirty yards distant from the enemy. Several cases are remembered of poor lads who stumbled exhausted and were drowned in that awful mire.

Against that background Haig decided to make one last push against Beaucourt and Beaumont Hamel, a first-day objective which had come to be regarded by both sides as being impregnable. The attack was due to begin on 24 October, but after many postponements finally commenced on 13 November with the explosion of a mine in front of the German lines and the customary artillery barrage. Under the command of Major-General George 'Uncle' Harper the 51st (Highland) Division attacked with two brigades and one in reserve, using 'leap-frog' tactics as they advanced towards the German lines of defence. On the right, 1/6th Black Watch and 1/7th Gordons quickly reached the German front line and took it without difficulty and although 1/8th Argylls and 1/5th Seaforths were checked on the left by heavy German machine-gun fire, they were able to fight their way through to the second line. One platoon of 1/8th Argylls, led by Lieutenant W.D. Munro, succeeded in capturing a German battalion headquarters and its inhabitants. The men's initiative had been greatly assisted by the earlier capture of German maps detailing the enemy's positions. Harper's tactics worked in that the division achieved its objectives with only 2,200 casualties, killed, wounded or missing. To the soldiers this was a source of great satisfaction, as the failure to take High Wood had attracted to them the unattractive nickname of 'Harper's Duds' – a play on their HD divisional badge. All that changed after the assault on Beaumont Hamel. As Harper watched the walking wounded making their way back to the line two days later he overheard one of his Jocks remarking: 'Onyway, they winna ca' us Hairper's Duds noo.' From that point onwards the 51st (Highland) Division was held in high regard by the Germans as one of the crack infantry formations in the British Army.

During the fighting on the Somme, which lasted five months, the Allies lost over 613,000 casualties, two-thirds of them British, while the German losses cannot have been much less. (These are difficult to compute as they did not include wounded who were expected to survive.) In the cold statistical analysis of modern warfare the Allies did better out of the battle than the Germans, and most modern military historians are agreed that it was 'a win on points'. Although the expected breakthrough never occurred and the six miles of crescent-shaped ground gained was a modest return for the expenditure of so many lives and so much materiel, pressure had been taken off the French and valuable lessons had been learned. After the war senior German commanders complained that the Somme was 'the muddy grave of the German field army', while their opposite numbers in the British Army argued that their inexperienced divisions came of age during the battle, even though most of the lessons were bloodily learned. Long after the operational phase of the battle had ended Captain John Lauder, 1/8th Argylls, was killed near Courcellete on 28 December. He was the son of the prominent entertainer Harry Lauder, who was told the news a few days later while appearing in the revue *Three Cheers* at the Shaftesbury Theatre in London. Ironically, one of the show's best known songs was 'The Laddies who Fought and Won'. Following John Lauder's death there were persistent rumours that he was an unpopular officer and had been shot in the back by his own men, although this is not borne out by letters his father received from other officers in the battalion.

GALLIPOLI

1/5th battalion

The stalemate on the Western Front encouraged thoughts of opening a second front, and the opportunity was provided by Turkey's entry into the war in December 1914. The target was Constantinople, capital of the Ottoman Empire, which could be attacked through the Dardanelles to allow a joint British and French fleet to enter the Black Sea following the destruction of the Turkish forts on the Gallipoli peninsula. At that point it would have been safe to land ground forces to complete the capture of the peninsula and to neutralise the Turkish garrison. However, the plan was stymied by the sinking of several Allied capital ships and a consequent loss of nerve in the high command. Following the failure of the naval operations to destroy the Turkish forts it was decided to land troops at Cape Helles on 25 April, but the landings were opposed by the Turks, who offered stout resistance. By the end of the month the British had suffered around 9,000 casualties, one-third the size of the attacking force, in return for little ground gained. Reinforcements were required and amongst them was

1/5th Argylls as part of 157 Brigade in 52nd (Lowland) Division, which began landing in the peninsula in the first week of June. The rest of the brigade consisted of three Territorial battalions of The Highland Light Infantry (1/5th, 1/6th, 1/7th).

After spending some time in the trenches to acclimatise and become used to the enervating operational conditions on the peninsula 157 Brigade first saw battle on 12 July, when it was used in the division's attack on an enemy position called Achi Baba Nullah. This had been a target from the outset but it was heavily defended by the Turks with a complicated system of trenches which were heavily wired. The task was entrusted to 155 Brigade on the extreme right of the position and to 157 Brigade on the left (156 Brigade which had already been in action acted as divisional reserve). In the first instance the guns of the Allied artillery would bombard the Turkish lines ahead of the assault on the right before turning their attention to the centre. Initially the two brigades were ordered to complete their advance once the first three lines of trenches had been captured, but this led to confusion in some areas where only two lines had been completed.

Following a massive bombardment which opened at 4.30 a.m. and ended three hours later the two Scottish brigades moved forward in four waves, with 1/5th Argylls in the centre of 157 Brigade's attack. Thanks to the accuracy and power of the Allied bombardment the Turkish lines had been devastated but confusion quickly set in when the troops became disorientated in the shambles. Although the two attacking brigades had succeeded in reaching their objectives there were delays in bringing up the reserves and the Scots found themselves caught up in the wreckage of the Turkish trenches. Given the heavy enemy fire and the difficult terrain, it was not surprising that things went wrong and the Turks were able to regroup. The following day 1/5th Argylls held a position known as 'the horseshoe', which quickly became a focus of Turkish counter-attacks. Support arrived in the shape of the Royal Naval Brigade, which suddenly and unexpectedly arrived in the Argyll trenches having crossed 500 yards over open ground under heavy fire. 'What the — do you want?' was the puzzled response of an Argyll officer as the survivors struggled into the horseshoe position. During the fighting at Helles the British lost 7,700 casualties between 21 June and 13 July. Of that number 333 were Argylls.

Serving in Gallipoli was not for the faint-hearted. Not only was the fighting conducted at close-quarters, with some trenches being almost in touching distance, but the physical hardships were worse than anything faced on the Western Front. Despite the best efforts at maintaining basic sanitation, disease was rampant, especially dysentery and enteric fever, which were spread by the absence of proper latrines and washing facilities and by the ever-present swarms of black, buzzing flies. In the heat of high summer the swarms were especially bad and even the advent of colder autumn weather brought little respite as the sun gave way to long days of freezing rain.

Despite the arrival of reinforcements – in all, the senior British commander General Sir Ian Hamilton was given five new divisions – the deadlock could not be broken and the men on the peninsula were becoming increasingly weakened. An ambitious amphibious landing at Suvla Bay failed in August because the Turks were able to rush reinforcements into the area to prevent the creation of a bridgehead. In October the inevitable happened: Hamilton was sacked, rightly so as his leadership had become increasingly feeble and sterile, and he was replaced by General Sir Charles Monro, a veteran of the fighting on the Western Front who was also a disciple of the westerners. Having taken stock of the situation he recommended evacuation, although this was not accepted until the beginning of November when Kitchener himself visited the battle-front and found himself agreeing that the difficulties were insuperable. In a brilliant operation, which was all the more inspired after the fiascos which had preceded it, the British finally withdrew their forces at the end of 1915, remarkably without losing any casualties. The great adventure to win the war by other means was finally over.

As happened on other fronts during the war the exact British death toll was difficult to compute, but most estimates agree that 36,000 deaths from combat and disease is not an unreasonable tally. The official British statistics show 117,549 casualties – 28,200 killed, 78,095 wounded, 11,254 missing. Total Allied casualties were put at 265,000. Most of the survivors were sent back to France in time to take part in the Battle of the Somme while others, including the 52nd (Lowland) Division were sent to Egypt to guard the Suez Canal and train for the forthcoming operations against Ottoman forces in Palestine and Syria.

MACEDONIA (SALONIKA)
1st and 12th battalions

The withdrawal from Gallipoli allowed the British and the French to build up forces in the Balkans, both to support Serbia and to prevent Bulgarian forces from influencing events in the region – on 5 October 1915 Bulgaria's army had been mobilised, and it entered the war on the side of the Central Powers. The Allied response was to send two divisions (10th Irish and 156th French) to the port of Salonika (Thessaloniki) under the command of the French General Maurice Sarrail. At the time German and Austro-Hungarian forces had invaded Serbia and had entered Belgrade while Bulgarian forces had pushed into Macedonia, a move which stymied any Allied attempt to relieve pressure on the Serbs. As a result Sarrail's divisions were pushed back into Salonika, which rapidly became a huge military base – by the end of the year three French and five British divisions together with a huge amount of stores and ammunition were encamped in a perimeter which was 200 miles square and defended by acres of barbed wire. For entirely political reasons, the British supported the deployment with five additional divisions (22nd, 26th, 27th, 28th and 60th), which the Germans ridiculed as 'the greatest internment camp in the world' and which prevented vital reinforcements and equipment from being deployed on the Western Front.

Amongst the 11 Scottish infantry regiments which took part in the campaign were 1st and 12th Argyll and Sutherland Highlanders but they did not see action until the summer of 1916, when British XVI Corps (Lieutenant-General C.J. Briggs) advanced up the valley of the River Struma towards the border with Bulgaria. The move was made to encourage Romania to join the war on the Allied side and most of the fighting was undertaken by the French divisions which had to face determined Bulgarian counter-attacks. Most of the British effort was confined to the Struma Valley, where the participants found that the style of fighting seemed to come from a different age. On 30 September three Scottish regiments of 81 Brigade – 1st Royal Scots, 2nd Camerons and 1st Argylls – moved across the Struma to attack Bulgarian positions in the fortified villages of Karajakoi Bala and Karajakoi Zir with the Royal Scots' pipers leading them into battle. In a memoir written by 2nd Lieutenant G.F. MacLean, C Company 1st Argylls, and deposited in the Liddle Archive at Leeds University, there is a lively description of the fighting to take the strongly held enemy position at Karajakoi Zir after Karajakoi Bala had been taken:

> C Company advanced, crossed the sunken road where the enemy outposts had been, turned right with our right on the road to make sure we would hit the enemy work . . . Captain Lothian, commanding, ordered the charge, the piper played the charge and the Jocks let out a terrific yell.

> The [Bulgarian] heavy machine-gun fired two bursts over our heads. It had us at its mercy. The machine-gunners must have seen by their flares 150 yelling bayonets descending upon them . . . The Bulgars fled into the village and the arms of the Camerons. There was nothing wrong with the heavy machine-gun, we turned it on the Bulgar officers riding for Seres to escape capture.

Both objectives were captured, with the loss of 1,248 casualties, and it was the biggest operation undertaken by British forces in Salonika in 1916. However, it was quickly becoming apparent that the main British losses were not battlefield casualties but men who fell victim to malaria – for every casualty from enemy action, ten found themselves in hospital as a result of illness and some units were unable to function. Dysentery and various enteric diseases also caused havoc and put a great strain on the medical services but malaria was a constant problem mainly because it was endemic in the area and proved difficult to eradicate. Re-infection was also a problem for although malaria did not kill men in great numbers – fatalities were confined to one per cent of hospital admissions – it did remove soldiers from operational service and in the worst cases incapacitated men had to be evacuated. The 1st battalion's average monthly admissions to hospital were 106, while the average monthly discharges were 35. 'Nothing that human ingenuity could devise could keep the disease in check,' noted the battalion's war historian. 'Salonika provides a striking contrast to Burma in the 1939–45 war, where the suppressive tablets, issued and taken daily by all ranks, rendered the incidence of malaria almost negligible, as far as the operations of the army were concerned, and this in a region probably more infested with the malaria-carrying anopheles than the Struma Valley.'

SEVEN

The First World War: 1917–19

No account of the regiment's war service on the Western Front can avoid any mention of Ian Hay's bestselling novel *The First Hundred Thousand*. The author's pen name disguised John Hay Beith, an officer in 10th Argylls who wrote for *Blackwood's Magazine* under another pseudonym, 'Junior Sub', in order to preserve his identity as a serving officer. A popular light novelist who had been educated at Fettes College in Edinburgh, where he also worked for a time as a master, Beith volunteered at the beginning of the war and was commissioned in The Argyll and Sutherland Highlanders, serving in the first of its New Army service battalions. By November the first of a series of his sketches appeared in *Blackwood's* with an account of the tribulations of learning close-order drill and throughout the autumn and winter Junior Sub's musings took the reader through the training of the fictional battalion referred to as the thinly disguised 'Bruce and Wallace Highlanders' until it was ready to cross over to France to go into action.

Brilliantly conceived and narrated in the first person and present tense, Beith's creation was akin to a homely correspondence and the sketches became an immediate bestseller when they were published in December 1915 under the title *The First Hundred Thousand* with the author listed as 'Ian Hay'. This was also an intensely Scottish account, seen from the perspective of a man who, though born in England, was deeply proud of his heritage, telling his readers early on 'we are Scotsmen, with all the Scotsman's curious reserve and contempt for social airs and graces'. Beyond that, the novel also provided a keen insight into the military mind, so much so that many brigade and divisional commanders recommended it as reading matter for their newly joined officers. For readers at home it was an accurate portrayal of the enthusiasm and optimism of those early days before the New Army divisions first went into action at Loos. So highly esteemed was Hay's creation within the regiment that in the introduction to the war history of 10th Argylls, Hay's battalion, Lieutenant-Colonel H. G. Sotheby reminded his readers that the first draft had already been written in *The First Hundred Thousand*.

WESTERN FRONT
2nd, 1/5th, 1/6th, 1/7th, 1/8th, 10th, 11th and 14th battalions

Early in 1917, the German high command decided to shorten the line between Arras and the Aisne by constructing new and heavily fortified defences which would be their new 'final' position behind the Somme battlefield. Known to the Allies as the Hindenburg Line, this formidable construction shortened the front by some 30 miles and created an obstacle which would not be taken until the end of the war. The withdrawal began on 16 March and as the Germans retired they laid waste to the countryside, leaving a devastated landscape in which the cautiously pursuing Allies had to build new trench systems. The new situation led to proposals for a new Allied attack on the shoulders of the Somme Salient, with the French attacking in the south at Chemin des Dames while the

British and Canadians would mount a supporting offensive at Arras and Vimy Ridge. Prior to the British attack there would be a huge and violent bombardment, with 2,879 guns firing 2,687,000 shells over a five-day period, making it heavier and more lethal than the barrage that had preceded the Somme in the previous summer. The Battle of Arras involved seven battalions of The Argyll and Sutherland Highlanders (2nd, 1/6th, 1/7th, 1/8th, 10th, 11th and 14th). They were part of the force of 44 Scottish infantry battalions (out of 124) which took part in the fighting in April 1917. Unfortunately, due to the demands of the war industries in the west of Scotland, shortage of recruits in Dumbartonshire meant that the 1/9th battalion ceased to exist following its shortlived amalgamation with the 1/7th battalion.

The Battle of Arras began in the early morning of 9 April 1917 in a biting wind which sent snow flurries scudding across the countryside, but despite the wintry weather the portents were good. For the first time the assault battalions found that the artillery had done their job by destroying the wire and new types of gas shells had fallen in the rear areas, killing German transport horses and making the movement of guns impossible. Within a few hours the German line had been penetrated to a depth of two miles, and in one of the most astonishing feats of the war the Canadian divisions swept on to take the previously impregnable German positions on the gaunt features of Vimy Ridge. The first day of the assault was a triumph for the British and the Canadians, who succeeded in taking their first objectives and then regrouping to attack the second and third lines of defence. The first phase of the battle encouraged hopes that this might be the long-awaited breakthrough and some units were surprised both by the ease of their attack and the lack of German resistance. For example, all the Argyll battalions achieved their first day objectives: the 1/7th battalion enjoyed the heady sensation of advancing to within striking distance of Bailleul, while at Rolincourt 1/8th Argylls succeeded in taking the second and third German lines. In another position, the Argylls succeeded in capturing a German regimental command and his headquarters staff. But it was at this point that things began to fall apart.

A blizzard swept across the battlefield and this caused immediate problems for the attacking soldiers, who had been ordered to leave their greatcoats behind. There were also problems coordinating the creeping barrage which allowed the infantrymen to advance under a measure of protection – some formations moved forward so quickly that they found themselves coming under friendly fire from their own guns. As the war historian of 1/7th Argylls noted, it was all an uphill struggle: 'Tired men staggered rather than marched along, chilled in every limb, their feet and kilts heavy with mud and slush.' Serving in 152 Brigade, the 1/8th battalion had managed to take its objectives but success came at a cost: when it was eventually relieved its fighting strength had been reduced to five officers and 200 soldiers. Total casualties were 670 killed or wounded. For the 10th battalion it was a similar story. Although it achieved its objectives in a brigade attack which saw it leap-frogging through 8th Black Watch and 7th Seaforth Highlanders it, too, became bogged down and two rifle companies were effectively destroyed.

Despite those problems the British commander directing the battle, General Sir Edmund Allenby, ordered the attack to be resumed with an assault on the final German line, the Green Line, at Monchy. He was optimistic of success, but already the opposing German commander in the Arras–Vimy sector, General Ludwig von Falkenhausen, had started moving his reserves from their pre-battle positions 15 miles behind his lines. At headquarters Haig urged Allenby to keep up the momentum, believing that a rupture was imminent, and spurred on by his commander-in-chief Allenby urged his men to press on with the next phase of the battle and to 'understand that the Third Army is now pursuing a defeated enemy and that risks must be freely taken'. Monchy fell on 12 April, but time was fast running out for the ever more exhausted assault battalions. Increased German resistance and reinforcement meant higher casualties for the attackers, and so it proved. On 15 April, almost a week after the first attack, Haig succumbed to reason and to the pleas of three divisional commanders and called a halt to the first phase of the battle to allow reinforcements to be brought up.

This time there were to be no easy gains and the British attack soon faltered as the assault battalions came up against stronger German opposition, leaving the historian of the 9th (Scottish) Division to lament: 'Little can be said in defence of this battle, which the Division fought with great reluctance. The preparations and arrangements were hurried to a deplorable degree.' Later in the battle, during the assault on the River Scarpe, the 2nd battalion lost eight officers killed and six wounded, 53 soldiers killed and 144 wounded, while 77 were missing presumed killed. In one incident, one of its rifle companies had been isolated with a rifle company of the 1st Middlesex but had been able to hold out long enough for reinforcements to reach them. For men who had been in continuous action in the first phase of the battle, this second assault along the Scarpe proved to be a battle too far, and five days later Allenby was forced to scale down the offensive. Some of the fiercest fighting was at Roeux and its ill-famed chemical works, which had been captured briefly by the 51st (Highland) Division, only for it to be retaken by the Germans. On 28 April, a fresh assault on the village was made by 34th Division, and in common with other operations at this stage of the battle it was hurried and improvised. The preceding artillery barrage failed to unsettle the German defenders, who were in the process of rushing reinforcements into the village for an attack of their own. The *Official History* referred to Roeux simply as 'a melancholy episode', while the historian of the 1/7th battalion noted grimly:

> In the later days of the war, when the [Highland] Division
> passed that way, many significant glances were directed to
> the ill-fated red-brick ruins of the chemical factory, the
> fighting for which had cost so many splendid lives.

Arras is not one of the better known battles of the First World War but it deserves to be remembered for a number of reasons. The initial attacks demonstrated that the British had learned from the Somme by concentrating their artillery to pin down the enemy in his deep trenches and make life easier for the attacking infantry. The barrage was also more accurate and proved to be more effective against wire. On the first day the advance took the attackers up to three miles into German territory, with the 4th Division leap-frogging over the 9th (Scottish) Division to make one of the biggest single advances made by infantrymen fighting on the Western Front. For the Canadians, supported by 51st (Highland) Division, the first day was even more spectacular: after taking the Vimy Ridge they looked down on to the Douai plain and saw the Germans in full retreat. Casualties on the first day were one-third of those suffered in the comparable period on the Somme, and large numbers of German prisoners had been taken. From the point of objectives being reached and casualties kept down, the first day of fighting at Arras deserves to be called a 'triumph'. Thereafter matters did not run so smoothly and the impetus was lost. Bad weather was one reason – the snow and rain did not make life easy for the men on the ground and delayed the transport – but it proved impossible to sustain the attack with exhausted troops. Any opportunity for an early breakthrough was lost when the Germans pushed reinforcements into the line, and their arrival quickly nullified Allenby's earlier tactical advantage.

By the time that the fighting ended at the beginning of May, any hope of defeating the Germans at Arras had disappeared and the losses had multiplied. The British suffered around 159,000 casualties, a daily rate of 4,076 (higher than the Somme's 2,943), and the stuffing had been knocked out of many of the formations which had been involved in a month of hard fighting against a heavily reinforced enemy. Given that so many Scottish battalions were involved in the fighting, roughly a third, a high proportion of the casualties were Scots; one brigade in the 51st (Highland) Division lost 900 casualties in the final and bloodiest phase of the battle, the majority being killed or wounded by shrapnel. During the fighting the 1/7th battalion's losses were 12 officers killed and 11 wounded, 86 soldiers killed and 359 wounded.

For the Argyll battalions most of the summer was spent in reserve and taking their turn in the line. The 2nd battalion returned to Boyelles in the Ypres sector while the 1/7th and 1/8th battalions moved to St Omer before holding the line on the River Steenbeck, also in the Ypres sector. Warfare is not just about action; it also involves periods of tedium or days when nothing in particular happens. An entry in the War Diary of the 11th battalion gives some idea of the conditions experienced by those serving with 45 Brigade on the Ypres front in the summer of 1917:

10 July 1917

Owing to circumstances relief was not completed till 3:45am. Strict orders of necessity of little movement by day – greatly hampers work. Night reorganisation of front line Companies. Burial of dead. Clearing up of Piccadilly Trench (scene of barrage on night of 9/10th). Work hampered by large parties bringing up Livens Gas

Projectors. Large numbers of working parties away from trenches. This practically did away with any support or reserve, leaving some 190 all ranks to hold battalion front. This grave danger is a source of complaint to Brigade. Hostile aeroplane about 8:30pm, about 3–400 feet up, controlled enemy 5.9 fire. No retaliation from our aircraft.

The next battle involving the regiment was the Third Battle of Ypres, better known as Passchendaele, which opened in July 1917 and continued for four months. Prior to the battle 1/7th and 1/8th Argylls made extensive preparations to study the ground over which they would be fighting, even going to the extent of preparing a miniaturised version on clay soil near Poperinghe known as 'A 30, Central'. Wooden standards marked the boundaries, while printed notice-boards indicated the salient features – farms, woods, rivers and so on – and the main up-and-down routes were also clearly indicated, to allow the men to familiarise themselves with the battlefield. Further steps were taken to give the attacking battalions the best possible chance of making their way forward when the division went into the attack at 5.40 a.m. on 20 September:

To avoid the possibility of mistake, one directing post per half platoon was made and set up in position some hours before the [1/7th] Battalion assembled. These consisted of wooden stakes to which tin discs were fastened, the discs having been treated with blue luminous paint on one side only, so as to be visible to anyone approaching our front line from the rear. The stakes were rendered identifiable by a system of tangible strips of leather so that each half-platoon could identify its own. Each stake, moreover, was so placed that an arrow fixed to the side indicated the line of advance.

> The Battalion formed up on these directing posts with
> the most admirable accuracy. The whole battle, indeed,
> was a triumph of organisation and everything happened
> according to plan.

By then 1/8th Argylls had already been in action in a well-planned and successful attack in the opening days of the battle in July. Again, careful preparation before the assault kept casualties to a minimum, the battalion War Diary noting that instead of using a 'wild and expensive charge' the attacking infantry made 'skilful use of ground'. Further to the north, between the salient and the English Channel coast, the 2nd battalion was part of the flanking force which had been deployed to exploit any breakthrough, but when that possibility failed to materialise it was moved to the Hooge sector. During the September assault the 2nd battalion was involved in the operations to take Polygon Wood as part of an offensive to take the Menin Road Ridge. Aided by a huge artillery bombardment, the attacking forces gained ground but the deteriorating conditions left a toll on the men. In the opening minutes of the battle to take Passchendaele on 12 October there was heavy rain and the War Diary of 10th Argylls noted that 'every man was drenched to the skin and very cold'. The diarist of the 11th battalion voiced the thought that conditions were worse than on the Somme in the previous year but the men remained 'alert and cheerful in spite of a night of incessant rain'. By the time the fighting petered out towards the end of the year the ground gained on the salient stretched as far as Poelcapelle and Passchendaele but the casualty list was predictably large: 310,000 dead and wounded.

Before the year ended the 14th battalion was involved in the Battle of Cambrai, the first time that tanks were used on a large scale. It was largely a failure due to the inexperience of the supporting infantry and weaknesses in command, but it pointed the way to the kind of battle that would be fought in the latter stages of the war. During the fighting 14th Argylls was part of 40th Division's attack on Bourlon Wood to the west of the town of Cambrai. The new year was only three months into its stride when the Germans launched their biggest counter-attack of the war. The storm broke in the early hours of the morning of 21 March 1918 when the German artillery produced a huge bombardment which lasted for five hours and which left the defenders badly shaken and disorientated. Gas and smoke shells added to the confusion, which was increased by an early morning mist, leaving commanders with no exact idea of where and when the infantry attack was coming. In their defensive positions in the Cambrai sector near Beaumetz the 51st (Highland) Division had its first inkling that something was afoot when scouting parties observed thousands of German infantrymen entering the front-line trenches carrying weapons but leaving behind their heavy packs, clearly preparing for an assault.

In the first minutes C company of 1/8th Argylls was wiped out and the battalion was forced to retire with 542 casualties while 1/7th Argylls, in reserve at the time, had to fight for its very existence, as did every battalion in the division, which lost three out of ten battalion commanders while over 20,000 soldiers went into captivity. On the Arras sector held by XVII Corps the brunt of the German attack fell on the 15th (Scottish) Division south of the Scarpe and the divisional commander, Major-General Hamilton Lyster Reed, VC, a gunner, was told by his superiors in no uncertain terms that there was to be no withdrawal and no surrender: 'The Division is now in a point of honour. The ground it holds is of the utmost importance and it is to be held at all costs.' A diary entry for 28 March made by Robert Lindsay Mackay, a young officer in 11th Argylls, tells its own story:

Wakened up after two hours' sleep at 3 a.m. by deuce of a bombardment. The very earth seemed to tremble, just as at Ypres last year. Gas shells in hundreds came over, and the back areas got a big share. In the darkness we could do nothing but wait on the dawn. All our lines, both forward and back, became broken. Bombardment of our lines kept up by Boche for three hours.

In the later stages of the German assault the 2nd battalion was involved in fighting at Metern while the 14th battalion took part in the defence of Guemappe. By the beginning of April the Germans had advanced 20 miles along a 50-mile front, creating a huge bulge in the Allied line, and had pushed themselves to within five miles of Amiens. However, despite the heavy Allied losses, the Germans had shot their bolt and while they managed to capture a huge salient they too had suffered huge losses – as many as 250,000 men – and by the end of April the Germans' spring offensive came to an end. Following its failure the Germans turned their attention to the French armies along the Aisne. Once again the German assault forces achieved an initial success by breaching the opposition's defences and by 30 May they had reached the Marne, creating a salient 20 miles deep and 30 miles wide. Vigorous counter-attacks frustrated the German advance and British forces were also involved when the newly formed XXII Corps under Lieutenant-General Sir Alexander Godley were deployed in support of the French Army in Champagne. Amongst its four divisions were 15th (Scottish) and 51st (Highland) and both of them took part in what became known as the Second Battle of the Marne, which finally halted the German advance in the middle of July. During the fighting 11th Argylls found itself serving alongside French and US soldiers, but as Mackay's diary makes clear Allied cooperation only went so far:

Have been much impressed on these marches by the salutes
and greetings of the American and French soldiers. The
former were fascinated by our bag-pipes. Lord! How we
held our heads up high and stepped out when THEY were
watching, just to show them that we – WE – were winning
the war – and then the Americans would fall behind – and
we would carry on for another ten bloody miles without
speaking.

In the latter stages of the war 1/5th Argylls returned to France
as part of the reinforcement rushed to France as a result of the
German offensive (see below) and 1/6th Argylls returned to the
infantry role in the 51st (Highland) Division. At the same time, both
the 11th and 14th battalions were reduced to cadre strength before
being transformed into reinforcement formations, the second of
the two being reinforced by the 17th battalion. Applying relentless
pressure, the Allied advance continued throughout October and
into November as the Germans withdrew steadily back from their
positions on the Western Front. Familiar names were retaken –
for the British Le Cateau, for the French symbolic Sedan – and,
in common with other formations, the Argyll battalions found
themselves fighting over ground they had last seen years earlier.
Although the Germans were pulling back they still offered fierce
resistance and the Allies had to fight hard for every yard they gained.
For 1/5th Argylls this meant a first experience of fighting on the
Western Front at Kemmel Hill and Wytschaete Ridge in the Ypres
sector. For the 2nd battalion there was the disappointment of losing
A Company during the 33rd Division's attack on enemy positions
at Villers-Guislain and for 10th Argylls there were similar problems
at Joncourt, where 350 casualties were lost, killed and wounded.
Some idea of the regiment's overall losses on the Western Front
can be found in the experience of the 11th battalion. Between the

fighting on the Somme in 1916 and the Armistice in November 1918, 196 officers were posted to the battalion and of those 36 were killed in action or died of wounds. As the normal establishment for a battalion in those days was about 22–24 officers, 11th Argylls therefore renewed its whole officer strength some seven times in that period.

PALESTINE

1/5th battalion

Following the end of the Gallipoli campaign 1/5th Argylls was based in Egypt with 52nd (Lowland) Division prior to the opening of a new front against the forces of the Ottoman Empire in Palestine. The operation was entrusted to an Egyptian expeditionary force of 88,000 soldiers under the command of Allenby, who had been sacked after his failure at Arras in April 1917. Before taking up his new command he had been warned by Lloyd George that he had to take Jerusalem by Christmas as a gift to the British nation and that he should demand what he needed to make sure the enterprise succeeded. In fact there was already a pressing need to attack the Turkish forces, who were being reinforced in Aleppo in present-day Syria for an offensive to retake Baghdad. If Allenby could engage the enemy through Palestine it would force the Turks to divide their forces and pass the initiative back to the British.

From the outset Allenby recognised that he needed overwhelming superiority over the Turks if he were to avoid the setbacks at Gallipoli, but getting the reinforcements in the second half of 1917 was another matter. The priority continued to be the Western Front, and with the Battle of Passchendaele eating up resources it took time and much subtle diplomacy to build up his forces. Eventually these consisted of a Desert Mounted Corps made up of Anzac and British cavalry and yeomanry regiments and two infantry corps, one of which contained the 52nd (Lowland) Division, which had been moved to Egypt following the withdrawal from Gallipoli. Their objective was to break into Palestine through Gaza and Beersheba and destroy the defending Turkish Eighth Army.

Earlier in the campaign, in April and May, the British had failed to dislodge the Turkish positions in Gaza and had lost over 6,000 casualties in so doing, most of them suffered by the 52nd (Lowland) Division, but they got their revenge in the third battle, which opened on 31 October and ended on 7 November when the Turks were forced to retire. Following good work by the Australian cavalry the decisive strike was made at Sheria, where the enemy was quickly outflanked and forced to retire. One of the key units in the assault was 157 Brigade, containing 1/5th Argylls, and its courage and resolve was witnessed by W. T. Massey, the official war correspondent with Allenby's forces:

> The 157th Brigade in the early evening attacked the ridge and gained the whole of their objectives by eight o'clock. There ensued some sanguinary struggles on this sandy ground during the night. The Turks were determined to have possession of it and the Scots were willing to fight it out to a finish. The first counter-attack in the dark hours drove the Lowlanders off, but they were shortly afterwards back on the hills again. The Turks returned and pushed the Highland Light Infantry and Argyll and Sutherland Highlanders off a second time. A third attack was delivered with splendid vigour and the enemy left many dead, but they renewed their efforts to get the commanding ground and succeeded once more. The dogged Scots, however, were not to be denied. They re-formed and swept up the heavy shifting sand, met the Turk on the top with a clash and knocked him down the reverse slope. Soon afterwards there was another ding-dong struggle. The

Turks, putting in all their available strength, for a fourth time got the upper hand, and the Lowlanders had to yield the ground, doing it slowly and reluctantly and with the determination to try again. They were Robert Bruces, all of them. It's the best that stays the longest. After a brief rest these heroic Scots once more swarmed up the ridge. Their cheers had the note of victory in them, they drove their bayonets home with the haymakers' lift, and what was left of the Turks fled helter-skelter down the hill towards Deir Sineid, broken, dismayed, beaten, and totally unable to make another effort.

To great acclaim Jerusalem city fell on 8 December after a determined attack by the 53rd and 60th Divisions forced the remaining defenders to evacuate their positions. Three days later, in a carefully stage-managed operation, Allenby and his staff entered the city to take possession of it and to secure the holy places. It was not the end of the war in Palestine but it was the beginning of the end. Allenby's next objectives were to move into Judea and to regroup to prevent Turkish counter-attacks before moving on to his next objectives, Beirut, Damascus and Aleppo. However, to accomplish that he would need additional troops to reinforce his own men and to protect the lines of communication as he pushed north; at the very least, he told the War Office, he would need an additional 16 divisions, including one of cavalry. In the short term his forces invested Jaffa, which fell after the 52nd (Lowland) Division seized the banks of the River Auja in an operation which demanded surprise and, according to the divisional War Diary, resulted in 'the most furious hand-to-hand encounters of the campaign'. At the height of the battle 1/5th Argylls moved forward to within 20 yards of the enemy before clearing the enemy positions with a determined bayonet charge.

This proved to be the last action undertaken by the majority of the Scottish regiments in Palestine. Before the question of reinforcing Allenby could be addressed by the War Office the Allies were faced by the crisis on the Western Front in March 1918, when a German offensive pushed back the British line some 40 miles between Arras and La Fère, the old Somme battlefield. The need for rapid reinforcement came at the very moment when Allenby wanted to continue the push towards Aleppo and he was forced to order two infantry divisions, nine yeomanry regiments and one divisional artillery unit to move to France in March 1918. One of the divisions was 52nd (Lowland), which embarked for Marseilles at Alexandria aboard seven troopships escorted by six Japanese destroyers.

MACEDONIA (SALONIKA)
1st and 12th battalions

The last major actions in Salonika took place in May 1917 with an operation by the French and Serb forces to break through the Bulgarian defensive lines. The British objectives, undertaken by XII Corps, were the heavily defended positions to the west of Lake Doiran but the Allied offensive failed and had to be abandoned on 23 May with the loss of 5,024 British casualties. As had happened on the Western Front, the Allied artillery failed to cut the wire and the attacking infantry soon found themselves pinned down by accurate Bulgarian artillery and machine-gun fire. However, the enemy also proved to be surprisingly inefficient, with dilapidated trenches and straggling barbed wire emplacements which seemed to have been thrown into position without any care. In some places around the village of Homondos in the Struma Valley, which was attacked on 12–13 October, the defences were much less formidable than had been anticipated.

The mountainous terrain also helped the defenders and the

commander-in-chief of British Salonika Forces, Lieutenant-General G.F. Milne, was forced to concede that 'our men are not a match for the Bulgar in hill fighting, though superior on the flat'. (Other problems came from manpower shortages, lack of reliable equipment, especially heavy artillery, and the absence of coherent plans.) For the rest of the year the front remained surprisingly quiet while XVI Corps' activities in the Struma Valley were confined to a series of limited operations which were often little more than skirmishes with an increasingly reluctant enemy.

During the winter Greece finally entered the war on the Allied side following the abdication of the pro-German King Constantine, and at last the Allies were rewarded for their long-standing military presence in Salonika. At the same time Sarrail was sacked and replaced first by General M.L.A. Guillaumat and then by General Franchet D'Esperéy, who brought the campaign to a conclusion in the summer of 1918. Weakened by German troop withdrawals, the Bulgarian army failed to halt the last assault of the war, which began on 15 September and ended a fortnight later when the Bulgarian front was split. Known as the Second Battle of Doiran, the Allies launched 200,000 in the attack on the much-weakened enemy lines, with the British leading the flank attack with the Greeks on Strumitza to the east. A curiosity of the operation was the decision to use 'portable fires', rag bundles soaked in paraffin which were used to clear trenches suspected of containing gas shells. Another innovation was the use of shiny tin discs which every soldier carried to send signals to aircraft flying overhead in order to mark the position of the attackers. The 12th battalion's War Diary recorded how the system worked:

> Contact aeroplane test carried out. After station call acknowledged by plane several messages sent out. Plane then flew along a line where the platoon were extended

to represent assaulting troops. As plane approached men flashed tin discs in the sun. Plane acknowledged signal – few minutes later dropped a message containing a sketch showing position occupied by platoon.

Within two days the Serb forces had pushed the enemy back by almost 20 miles, but there were problems on the British flank where 77 Brigade came under heavy enemy fire from positions known as The Tongue, The Knot and The Tassel. Fighting alongside 8th Royal Scots Fusiliers, 12th Argylls endured heavy enfilading fire which prevented them from getting close to their final objective. In the War Diary Captain J.K. Matheson described the conditions which led the commanding officer, Lieutenant-Colonel Falconar Stewart, to order a withdrawal to The Tongue in order to regroup with the other two battalions:

> Two enemy machine-guns in position in a concealed concrete emplacement . . . opened fire traversing fire along our line as the assaulting waves approached The TONGUE and this accompanied by a TM [trench mortar] barrage severely depleted our ranks and caused the attack to waver. Capt J. Harvey Loutit and the other officers who accompanied the assaulting waves seeing what was about to happen quickly rallied the men and led them forward. But again owing to casualties they were forced to withdraw.

A similar fate met 11th Scottish Rifles, which at one point was reduced to throwing rocks at the enemy due to an acute shortage of ammunition. By then the brigade had become increasingly isolated and the smoke and dust created by the artillery fired prevented them from giving or receiving messages to divisional headquarters. Men were becoming increasingly exhausted and, critically, were running out of ammunition. In the chaos, and expecting a Bulgarian counter-attack, Brigadier-General W.A. Blake took the decision to retire and to abandon the position, with the battalions being ordered to make good their escape as best they could carrying their wounded and their equipment. Both the Scots Fusiliers and the Scottish Rifles managed to pull out but in the mayhem of the noise of battle and the thick clouds of smoke and dust 12th Argylls stumbled into a Bulgarian position with predictable results:

> Strong parties of the enemy emerged from the WARREN and under cover of the smoke endeavoured to cut off our withdrawal. So dense was the smoke and dust that these parties . . . were in amongst our men before they were aware of the attack and many including the Commanding Officer were surprised and made prisoners. 2 men who subsequently escaped state that the party to which they belonged after being disarmed by the enemy were shot in cold blood by the Bulgarian soldiers and it was only the intervention of an officer which saved them from a similar fate.

Eventually the survivors reached the safety of Jackson's Ravine and were able to make their way back to the British support lines. During the operation 12th Argylls lost 50 per cent of its fighting strength, a significant percentage of the 7,103 British casualties killed and wounded. It was the last major battle of the campaign. On 29 September French forces entered Skopje and the following day Bulgaria requested an armistice. D'Esperéy was keen to continue his advance up through the Balkans to threaten Germany's southern flank and his troops were already crossing the Danube when the war came to an end on 11 November. At the same time Milne moved his British forces up to the Turkish frontier, but his hopes of attacking Turkey ended when the Turks signed an armistice on 31

October. Elements of British forces remained in the area into 1919, serving as peacekeepers, and for most of them it was a dispiriting end to a campaign which had tied up huge numbers of men and materiel for no obvious strategic gains. Although the British Salonika Force listed a modest 18,000 casualties from combat, this was overshadowed by the 481,000 who had succumbed to illness, mainly malaria. To put those figures in a regimental perspective, between 1914 and the end of the fighting in 1918 the total losses in The Argyll and Sutherland Highlanders amounted to 413 officers and 6,475 soldiers killed in action on all battle-fronts.

EIGHT

The Second World War: 1939–42

Following the cessation of hostilities in November 1919, Britain's huge wartime armed forces started disbanding. In the army, while the Regular regiments remained in being the special service battalions of the New Armies were broken up and the Territorial battalions were also reduced in size – in 1921 the 5th/6th was formed on amalgamation of the two battalions and the wartime 16th battalion was disbanded. The 7th, 8th and 9th battalions remained intact. The regiment also changed its title in 1920, becoming The Argyll and Sutherland Highlanders (Princess Louise's). Not that there was an immediate return to peacetime conditions. For the 2nd battalion there was an arduous tour of duty in Ireland during the civil war (known variously as the Anglo-Irish War or War of Independence) which preceded independence in 1921. It was a squalid little conflict with murders and revenge killings carried out by both sides, the Irish Republican Army (IRA) as well as the security forces. 'The whole country runs with blood,' said a leader in the *Irish Times* on 20 April 1921. 'Unless it is stopped and stopped soon every prospect of political settlement and material prosperity will perish and our children will inherit a wilderness.' It was not until the end of 1921 that a political solution was imposed on the country and its warring factions, but the decision to keep the six Ulster counties separate from the Irish Free State was to cause equally vexing problems later in the century.

This was followed by extensive tours of duty in overseas stations. In 1927 the battalion moved to the West Indies followed by a deployment in Shanghai as part of a garrison of 11,000 British and Indian troops which had been stationed in northern China to protect British interests and investments against attack by local warlords. Following a shorter stay in Hong Kong, 2nd Argylls moved to India in 1933 where the pace of life in the British garrison was still leisurely and barely affected by the growing calls for independence. There were two tours of duty which took the battalion back to the stamping grounds of the old 93rd. In 1935 2nd Argylls joined a column in the Mohmand province and two years later was involved in operations against forces led by Mirza Ali Khan, the mettlesome Faqir of Ipi, a religious leader who had been fomenting trouble in the North-West Frontier Province and was rumoured to be holed up in a complex of caves at Arsal Kot in the Shaktu Valley. To bring him to book a column was formed under the command of Major-General A.F. Hartley, who decided to mount a diversionary attack using the Bannu Brigade, made up of 2/11th (Ludhiana) Sikhs, 1/17th Dogras, 2/4th Gurkha Rifles and 2nd Argylls. Accompanying the column were the mountain guns of 7th and 9th Mountain Batteries and 12th Field Company Madras Sappers and Miners. Ahead of the column rode eight platoons of the South Waziristan Scouts, who moved at their own speed while the infantrymen were set a pace of one mile an hour.

The column set off on the night of 11–12 May 1937 and the going was hard, with a steep climb up to the ridge over slabs of rock and the constant fear of being ambushed. Serving in the 2/4th

Gurkhas was John Masters, later a fine novelist and the author of a classic volume of military autobiography, *Bugles and a Tiger*, and he remembered the heightened tensions with soldiers 'swearing in ten languages' as they made their way across the dark gullies. By dawn the first objective was reached and named Coronation Camp, it being the same day that George VI was being crowned in Westminster Abbey in faraway London. A week later, on 18 May, the column pushed on to Arsal Kot and after a fierce fire-fight with the Faqir of Ipi's forces the cave system was captured and then blown up. During the fighting the battalion lost 13 men 'due to their own incompetence' wrote Captain (later Brigadier) W.A. Gimson of the Tochi Scouts, but that was the voice of an officer who served in an elite regiment and had long experience of the frontier and the Pushtu tribesmen. More in keeping with the mood was Masters' carefully observed description of a conversation between a Gurkha soldier and an Argyll (the commanding officer's soldier-servant) who sat for an hour in the sun talking:

> I wondered what medium they were using for communication, since Rifleman Janaksing Thapa spoke no English and I doubted that Private Donald Campbell had much Gurkhali. I crept closer and stretched my ears. Each soldier was speaking his own language and using few gestures – it was too hot on the rocks for violent arm-waving. I could understand both sides of the conversation, the Gurkhali better than the 'English', and it made sense. Questions were answered, points taken, opinions exchanged, heads nodded and lips sagely pursed. When M.L. [Gurkha commanding officer] moved on, the two shook hands, and the Jock said 'Abyssinia, Johnny!' He had poor Janaksing there.

In August 1939 the battalion left India to join the garrison in Singapore where it formed part of 12 Indian Infantry Brigade. Its commanding officer was Lieutenant-Colonel Ian Stewart who had served in the battalion during the First World War and had been wounded in the first fighting at Le Cateau.

The 1st battalion had also spent part of the post-war period in India (1919–23) before moving to Egypt where it was based at Moascar, close to the Suez Canal. Like India, this should have been a quiet posting – Egypt had achieved independence in 1922 but was still very much under British suzerainty – but in 1924 trouble erupted at Khartoum in Sudan, where two battalions of Egyptian infantry mutinied and the 1st battalion was rushed south to restore order. Although Sudan was ostensibly a protectorate of Egypt and Britain, ultimate responsibility for its security lay with the latter, hence the need for the presence of 1st Argylls. During the main action on 27 November the battalion lost one officer and five soldiers killed and seven soldiers wounded. For his part in directing operations the acting commanding officer, Major J.R. Couper, was awarded the Distinguished Service Order (DSO).

Following the suppression of the trouble the battalion returned to Cairo on 17 January 1925 and the Citadel Barracks was to be its home until February 1928 when it returned to Britain on the troopship *Nevasa*. For the next 11 years the battalion was the Argylls' home-service battalion, stationed variously at Shorncliffe (1928–30), Edinburgh (1930–35), Tidworth (1935–37) and Aldershot (1937–39). In April 1939 it moved to Palestine to join the British garrison, becoming part of 14 Brigade in 8th Infantry Division. Amongst the highlights of this pre-war period was the appointment as regimental mascot of Cruachan, a Shetland pony stallion, the gift of Princess Louise in 1929. The name belongs to a prominent mountain in Argyllshire and is also the war cry of the Clan Campbell, of which the princess's husband, the Duke of

Argyll, was chief. The first mascot died on 11 April 1942 aged 20 and was succeeded in 1952 by Cruachan II. Looking to the future, Cruachan III joined the regiment in 1995.

While the 1st battalion was stationed in Aldershot it was obvious that another war in Europe was imminent. In Germany the Nazis had come to power under Adolf Hitler and their presumptuous territorial claims were soon trying the patience of the rest of Europe. In 1938 Prime Minister Neville Chamberlain seemed to have bought 'peace in our time' following his negotiations with Hitler in Munich, which gave the Germans a free hand in the Sudetenland and subsequently in Bohemia and Moravia. However, it proved to be the calm before the storm. Having signed a peace pact with the Soviet Union Hitler then felt free to invade Poland at the beginning of September 1939. Chamberlain, who would be replaced as prime minister by Winston Churchill the following year, had no option but to declare war – Britain and Poland were bound by treaty – but the country's armed forces were hardly in a fit condition to fight a modern war. The British Army could only put together four divisions as an expeditionary force for Europe, six infantry and one armoured division in the Middle East, a field division and a brigade in India, two brigades in Malaya and a modest scattering of imperial garrisons elsewhere. Years of neglect and tolerance of old-fashioned equipment meant that the army was ill-prepared to meet the modern German forces in battle, and British industry was not geared up to make good those deficiencies. Once again in the nation's history it seemed that Britain was going to war with the equipment and mentality of previous conflicts. Events in Poland quickly showed that Germany was a ruthless and powerful enemy whose Blitzkrieg tactics allowed them to brush aside lesser opposition: using armour and air power the Germans swept into the country, which fell within 18 days of the invasion, allowing Hitler to turn his attention to defeating France.

To meet the challenge the government made belated attempts to strengthen the armed forces. In the army this entailed a rapid expansion of the Territorial Army. The amalgamated 5th/6th battalions resumed their previous separate identities – 5th and 6th – and were re-rolled as machine-gun battalions but this was a prelude to a greater change. In 1941 the two battalions became, respectively, 91st Anti-Tank Regiment (Argyll and Sutherland Highlanders) Royal Artillery and 93rd Anti-Tank Regiment (Argyll and Sutherland Highlanders), Royal Artillery. Having been resurrected in Dumbarton in 1919, the 9th battalion was also converted to the artillery role, becoming 54th Light Anti-Aircraft Regiment, Royal Artillery. It consisted of 160 (Dumbarton) Battery, 161 (Alexandria) Battery and 162 (Helensburgh) Battery. The 7th and 8th battalions remained as infantry, as did their duplicates, the 10th and 11th battalions, while the 12th, 13th, 14th, 15th and 30th served as home defence battalions for all or part of the war.

For the two anti-tank regiments raised from the Argylls it proved to be a slow and frequently wearisome conversion thanks to the lack of suitable equipment. As the historian of the new 91st Regiment noted, by the end of 1941 it was anti-tank in name only, as it was still equipped with machine-guns. There were also problems with head-dress. As a gunner regiment of the Royal Artillery there were objections voiced in the War Office about officers and men continuing to wear the tam o'shanter, but these were resolved when the regiment was moved to the 15th (Scottish) Division, which insisted on all supporting arms wearing Scottish head-dress. The only concession was the removal of Argyll collar-dogs from the battle dress, but these were simply restored and reappeared at the end of the war. This was a vital point, as the regimental historian noted: 'morale might well have vanished, never to return [at the end of 1941], if the CO had not fought for it and for the retention and recognition of those seeming trivialities which were its outward and visible signs.' As to weapons, the regiment was first equipped with the obsolescent but elegant 2-pounder anti-tank gun and then with the more effective 6-pounder, which had a range of 5,500 yards. A later arrival was the M10 tank destroyer or 'Firefly' based on the US Sherman tank and equipped with a 17-pounder anti-tank gun which was used by 144 and 146 Batteries.

FRANCE

7th, 8th and 9th (54th LAA Regiment RA) battalions

On the outbreak of war the 51st (Highland) Division mobilised its Territorial Army battalions with 7th and 8th Argyll and Sutherland Highlanders forming 154 Brigade with 6th Black Watch under the command of Brigadier A.C.L. Stanley-Clark. The division was commanded by Major-General Victor Fortune and crossed over to France to join the British Expeditionary Force (BEF) at the end of January 1940. Shortly after arriving it was bolstered by the arrival of three regular battalions, with 1st Black Watch taking the place of 6th Black Watch in the Argylls brigade. From Le Havre the division moved into its concentration area before moving up to the Belgian border in the middle of March. Its next destination was the Saar area of Lorraine, where the three battalions of 154 Brigade were the first to go into the front line, the much-vaunted French Maginot Line consisting of trench systems and fortified emplacements. This was the period known as the 'phoney war' before the Germans attacked into France and young officers such as 2nd Lieutenant John Parnell, 7th Argylls, discovered the gulf between peacetime training and active service:

> On patrol we wore the absolute minimum and just had
> our weapons and little else so that we could move quickly
> and get through fences. We didn't have sub-machine guns
> like the fighting patrols; the only weapons we had were the

rifle and the Bren. I carried a revolver. It was only later, on the Somme, that I discovered how useless a revolver was and used a rifle instead. I don't think we blacked our faces or anything sophisticated like that, and we had no communications at all . . . We weren't exactly experienced soldiers at that stage.

The 9th battalion was also in France, with the BEF in its new role as anti-aircraft gunners protecting forward positions against enemy air attack. Things became especially hot after 10 May, when German land and air forces attacked across the Low Countries as a prelude to invading France. Taken aback by the ferocity and speed of the German advance into Belgium, the BEF began its long retreat back to the Channel ports and the eventual evacuation from the beaches at Dunkirk. In its role as a light anti-aircraft regiment the old 9th battalion helped to cover the retreat and eventually managed to reach the Channel coast, where its 12 Bofors guns were destroyed before embarkation back to Britain. During the retreat 162 Battery had become detached while protecting airfields in the vicinity of Rheims and did not get out of France until the following month.

While the BEF was involved in the great escape at Dunkirk the 51st (Highland) Division was deployed along a defensive line to the south-west of Abbeville near the mouth of the River Somme. Sixty miles away to the south-west lay the small port of St Valéry-en-Caux, with the road via Dieppe forming a southern boundary. Following the initial German onslaught the Highland Division had been compelled to withdraw towards the fortified positions in the French Maginot Line, but the speed of the German Army's armoured assault meant that it was cut off from the rest of the BEF and its fortunes were now tied firmly to the French Third Army under the command of General Besson. During this difficult period it became clear to the British high command that some elements in the French Army were considering suing for peace. As these included the commander-in-chief, General Maxime Weygande, and Marshal Philippe Pétain, the renowned commander of the First World War, the threat had to be taken seriously. Churchill was determined to keep France in the war at all costs, and that necessity was to play a part in determining the fate of the Highland Division. If the French were to sue for an armistice, as had been threatened, it would allow their powerful navy to fall into German hands and make an invasion of Britain more likely. At the same time, Churchill wanted to withdraw the bulk of the BEF, even though that decision gave the impression to the French that their Allies were pulling out and leaving them to their fate. As the 51st (Highland) Division continued to pull further back into Flanders, the political thinking in London was to have a decisive effect in what happened to them in the days ahead.

On 4 June the division supported a French attack made by the remnants of the French armoured and artillery forces along the Mareuil ridge to the south of Abbeville but although the French fought with great determination they were outnumbered and outgunned. This was the last full-scale Allied attack of 1940 in France, but even as it took place the last of the BEF was being picked up from the Dunkirk beaches. Whatever the outcome of the attack on the Mareuil ridge, the 51st (Highland) Division was now on its own, together with the remnants of the 1st Armoured Division. Neither of the Argyll battalions was involved, as 154 Brigade was guarding the left flank towards Saigneville, but they were caught up in the ferocious German counter-attack the following day along the line between the Somme and the Aisne. The overwhelming power of the offensive sealed the division's fate as it withdrew to the coast and the possibility of being picked up by the Royal Navy at Le Havre.

THE ARGYLL AND SUTHERLAND HIGHLANDERS

During the fighting at Franleu A and C Companies of 7th Argylls were quickly overrun, communications collapsed and the four rifle companies were unable to offer supporting fire. With casualties mounting, it quickly became clear that the battalion was incapable of creating a structured defence and by the end of the day on 5 June it had ceased to exist as a fighting entity. The battalion War Diary described it as 'the blackest day in the history of the battalion' and this was reflected in the casualties – 23 officers and 500 soldiers killed, wounded or taken prisoner. Amongst them was the commanding officer, Lieutenant-Colonel E.P. Buchanan. Only D Company made it to safety, joining up with A and C Companies of the 8th battalion, which had reached the coast at Ault. Together with other survivors they formed part of a new breakout group known as 'Arkforce' after the village of Arques-la-Bataille in which it was formed. Most of the units involved in the operation lacked the carriers and weapons used by the rest of the division, but Arkforce was helped by the German decision to bomb the fuel to create a huge smokescreen. On 15 June the Argyll survivors were evacuated, appropriately enough, on board the SS *Duke of Argyll*, an LMS railway ferry which normally operated the Heysham to Belfast route.

They were amongst the lucky ones, as together with 4th Black Watch and 6th Royal Scots Fusiliers they were the only formations of the division to make it back to Britain. To the end, Fortune hoped to pull his division out of Le Havre, but after almost two weeks of hard fighting, on 12 June he was forced to surrender to his opponents, the German 7th Panzer Division led by General Erwin Rommel. More than 10,000 British troops went into captivity at St Valéry-en-Caux; in the Highland areas of Scotland there were scarcely any families who were unaffected by the loss of the division. For those captured the war meant five long years in camps in Germany and Poland, where the men were given agricultural work or laboured in coal mines, a dispiriting fate for any soldier.

NORTH AFRICA, CRETE AND ERITREA

1st battalion

War came to the 1st battalion in Jenin in Palestine, where it formed the 2nd Middle East Reserve Brigade Group with 2nd Leicesters and 1st South Staffords which was due to deploy to Egypt. However, the move did not take place and the battalion remained in Palestine with 14 Infantry Brigade on internal security duties. While there 1st Argylls was reinforced by the arrival of two officers and 80 other ranks from the Rhodesian Army, but they quickly accepted and embraced the regiment's ethos and traditions. Training continued until September 1940, when the 1st battalion moved to join the 4th Indian Division (Major-General Noel Beresford-Peirse) for the defence of the Western Desert against the possibility of Italian attack. There it transferred to 16 Infantry Brigade and took part in its first fighting of the war at Sidi Barrani on 10 December when the battalion went into the attack with the tanks of 7th Royal Tank Regiment. In the resulting rout the Italians were completely destroyed: after three days of fighting 38,300 soldiers went into captivity and 73 tanks and 422 artillery pieces were captured. The losses to the Allies were 133 killed, 387 wounded and eight missing.

The 1st battalion remained in Egypt until May 1941 when it was rushed to Crete, whose defence was considered to be vital to Britain's interests in the Aegean and the Mediterranean. This became even more imperative the following spring after the Germans moved rapidly into Yugoslavia and then into Greece, forcing the retreat of all British and Commonwealth troops. Many of these were shipped to Crete but they arrived without their equipment, including artillery and ammunition which had been left behind in Greece. By the end of April there were 30,000 troops on Crete under the command of General Bernard Freyberg, a New Zealander whose plan centred on the need to defend the key points – the airfields at Heraklion, Retimo and Maleme and the main port at Suda Bay. During the fighting the battalion was again part of 14 Brigade, which was entrusted with the defence of the Heraklion sector, including its vital airfield. Having landed last, 1ˢᵗ Argylls was given the responsibility for Tymbaki on the south coast, where the infantrymen were supported by two Matilda tanks of 7th Royal Tank Regiment. The German attack began on 19 May and by the end of the day 5,000 German airborne troops had landed on Crete, either by parachute or by gliders towed by Ju 52 transport aircraft.

For a while the defenders put up spirited resistance – the Germans had underestimated the size of the British garrison – but the lack of air cover soon became apparent. On 21 May the airfield at Maleme fell into German hands and four days later Freyberg informed Wavell, now commanding the forces in the Middle East, that 'our situation here is hopeless'. Fearing another calamity, Churchill agreed to a withdrawal and the evacuation began on the night of 28/29 May. The evacuation was a mixed success, several Royal Navy warships were bombed and over 5,000 Allied soldiers were left behind, including 300 Argylls who went into German captivity. As a result, the battalion lost valuable officers and men and it took until the beginning of 1944 for it to be brought back to full fighting effectiveness. In the words of its commanding officer, Lieutenant-Colonel R.C.B. Anderson, 'the battalion was destined to pursue its lonely way over a very wide area of the Middle East, performing many and varied tasks, some dull and monotonous, but no less essential.' Apart from internal security duties in Egypt and Sudan, 1ˢᵗ Argylls' only experience of further operational service came in the second half of 1941, when it joined 26 East African Brigade during the campaign against Italian forces in Eritrea.

MALAYA

2nd battalion

On Sunday, 7 December 1941, Japan entered the war with its infamous pre-emptive air strike on the US Pacific Fleet's base at Pearl Harbor in Hawaii. This was followed in quick succession by further Japanese attacks on the islands of Guam, Wake and Midway while the Japanese Second Fleet escorted General Tomoyoku Yamashita's Twenty-Fifth Army to attack the north-west coast of the Malay peninsula. At the same time three Japanese divisions prepared to invade the British colony of Hong Kong. However, it was the collapse of Malaya and the surrender of Singapore on 15 February 1942 which caused the biggest dent to British pride and prestige in the region. Coupled with the concurrent invasion of Burma, the Japanese were suddenly in a position to threaten British interests in India, the 'Jewel in the Crown' of the country's imperial holdings.

This was to be one of the biggest disasters for the Allies at any stage in the war. Too late, the garrisons in Malaya and Singapore had been reinforced but mostly by raw and untried troops. In 1941 command had been assumed by Lieutenant-General Arthur Percival, who had divided the island into three sectors: the southern was held by two Malay and one Straits Settlement volunteer brigades, the western by 8th Australian Division and 44 Indian Infantry Brigade and the north by 9th and 11th Indian Divisions. Shortly before the Japanese attack 18th British Division arrived, but it took little part in the fighting. There was virtually no air cover and most of it was provided by obsolescent aircraft.

Although the fall of Singapore has become a byword for catastrophe in the history of the British Army, some regiments were more disciplined than others and gave a better account of themselves in the fighting. Amongst these was 2nd Argylls, which had arrived in August 1939 to form 12 Indian Infantry Brigade with 4/19th Hyderabad Regiment and 5/2nd Punjab Regiment. Before the outbreak of the Second World War the 2nd battalion had begun training for jungle fighting and this was intensified in 1940. Not that their efforts were appreciated by their superiors. In his memoirs Captain A.J.C. Rose remembered being assured by a staff officer in Malaya Command that 'if we were not drowned in the seasonal rains we would be decimated by malaria'. Fortunately the commanding officer, Lieutenant-Colonel Ian Stewart, was a tremendous enthusiast and his men were quickly nicknamed 'Jungle Beasts' on account of their ability to survive and thrive in the enervating conditions of the Malayan jungle. They also mastered the arts of manoeuvring the elderly but still effective Lanchester armoured cars equipped with two Vickers machine-guns.

The story of the fall of Singapore is soon told. During the first week of December 1941 the Japanese began the invasion of Malaya, landing at Kota Bahru on the north-east corner and rapidly thrusting south. During this phase the 2nd battalion was involved in delaying operations as part of the rearguard for 11th Indian Division and did not engage the Japanese until 17 December at Titi-Karangan, where Colonel Stewart ordered Pipe-Major McCalman to play the tune 'Gabaidh sin an rathad mhor' ('We'll take and keep the highway'). Later, Stewart recorded that not only was the tune appositely named but that it had been first played after the involvement of the Appin Stewarts at the Battle of Pinkie in 1547. During the fighting the battalion lost 11 casualties but killed at least 200 enemy thanks to the Japanese tactics of attacking in 'human waves' against superior and disciplined firepower.

As the Allied forces began their retreat there followed bruising encounters at Lenggong, Kota Tampan, Gopeng Dipang and Telok Anson which left the 2nd battalion exhausted and badly depleted. The fiercest fighting took place on the River Slim, where the Lanchester armoured cars were no match for the heavier enemy armour. At one stage the battalion was reduced to 94 effectives under the command of Major David Wilson. As stragglers came in the number increased to 250 men who were given the responsibility of guarding the causeway into Singapore. Many of those taken prisoner were either bayoneted or marched into captivity and, given the Japanese attitude to prisoners-of-war, they faced an uncertain future. At the end of the month Colonel Stewart returned to the battalion after a short spell in charge of 12 Brigade, and the battalion was reinforced by 210 Royal Marines who had managed to escape from the earlier sinking of the battleships HMS *Prince of Wales* and HMS *Repulse*.

Thus was born the composite infantry battalion which was christened the 'Plymouth Argylls', an apposite name given the regiment's associations with Plymouth, the city in which the marines were based. (The local football team is called Plymouth Argyle and its title could have been derived from the founders' admiration for the style of football played by the regiment when it was based in Plymouth in the 1880s. Another clue is that the team's dark green and blue strip mirrored the regiment's tartan, but an alternative derivation could have been the name of the public house in which the founders first met.) Stewart renewed intensive training but time was running out for the exhausted and demoralised remnants of the Allied armies. On 8 February the Japanese started crossing from Johore into Singapore territory and within three days had gained a substantial foothold as Percival's forces moved back into the perimeter. During this period the Plymouth Argylls moved north up the Bukit Timah Road towards the airfield at Tengah. Two days of intense fighting followed during which the Argylls and the marines came under heavy aerial bombardment and attack by Japanese medium tanks. On Friday, 13 February, the Japanese intensified their attacks by shelling the civilian areas and causing great damage and creating large numbers of casualties. By then it had become clear to Percival that further resistance was futile: water supplies were running low and a defensive battle would only cause unacceptable numbers of civilian casualties.

The order to surrender was given on 15 February and the remaining members of the Plymouth Argylls were marched into captivity in Changi Prison. Led by Piper Charles Stuart they marched along streets lined by hundreds of Allied soldiers who stood to attention as they passed, to salute their courage during those last desperate days of fighting. Later, Field Marshal Sir Archibald Wavell, the army's commander-in-chief, added his own words of praise:

> There was one battalion – a battalion of the Argyll and Sutherland Highlanders – commanded by a remarkable commanding officer – which he trained most intensively in jungle fighting. There was no doubt whatever that this battalion was as good as and better than any of the Japanese, and naturally this battalion did quite magnificent work until they were practically wiped out in the battle of the Slim River on 8 January after a gallant fight.

Some of the survivors managed to escape on board naval vessels or Chinese junks – 52 Argylls and 22 marines made it to Ceylon and amongst their number was Colonel Stewart, who had been unwillingly evacuated and was later promoted to command 144 Infantry Brigade. Of those who went into captivity, many were sent to work on the notorious Burma Road railway in Thailand. All told, the Argylls suffered 244 casualties killed in action and 184 as a result of disease and deprivation while in Japanese captivity. Astonishingly two soldiers in the battalion remained at large in Malaya, where they helped to train Malay and Chinese resistance fighters.

NORTH AFRICA

6th (93rd Anti-Tank Regiment RA), 7th and 8th battalions

As a result of the losses sustained in France and Malaya the regiment was forced to re-form its lost and depleted battalions. The 7th battalion was rebuilt from those men who had managed to escape from St Valéry and they were reinforced by men from the duplicate 10th battalion (for a spell it was styled 7/10th battalion.) Following its escape from St Valéry the 8th battalion was trained for amphibious operations and served first with the Royal Marine Division and then with 1 Guards Independent Brigade until February 1943. A new 2nd battalion rose from the ashes and was formed from the 15th battalion in May 1942. Later it became part of the 15th (Scottish) Division. Following the loss of the original 51st (Highland) Division at St Valéry a new 51st (Highland) Division was re-formed out of another equally distinguished Scottish formation, the duplicate 9th (Scottish) Division. It was renumbered as the 51st and given the famous HD divisional sign and quickly started building up its own *esprit de corps* with the divisional headquarters in Rothes, Banffshire under the command of Major-General Neil Ritchie, Black Watch. The Argylls' contribution was the 7th battalion, which was joined by 1st and 7th Black Watch in 154 Brigade. The battalion was commanded by Lieutenant-Colonel Lorne Campbell, an inspirational commander who was awarded the Victoria Cross during the campaign in North Africa (see Appendix).

During its working-up period the new division served on coastal defence duties before sailing from the Clyde in June 1942 to join the Eighth Army in North Africa. Due to wartime conditions and the submarine menace, the convoy sailed around the Cape of Good Hope and it proved to be a long and wearisome voyage which lasted 59 days. By then the Italians had been joined in the North African desert by the German Afrika Korps under the command of General Erwin Rommel and had seized the initiative in the desert.

Tobruk had fallen into enemy hands following a German and Italian offensive; Cairo was under threat and it seemed inevitable that another enemy assault would lead to the collapse of British power in North Africa. Morale was low and defeat seemed inevitable. At that point Churchill decided to change the command structure by appointing General Bernard Law Montgomery to take over the Eighth Army. It proved to be an inspired choice and the tempo of training quickly increased to adapt the soldiers to the very different conditions of the desert.

Montgomery showed a sure touch in directing his first battle – the Battle of Alamein – which began on 23 October and turned out to be the first decisive British land victory of the war. Not only did he bring scrupulous planning to the preparations but he also instilled a belief in the Eighth Army that they had the training and the equipment to defeat an enemy which was thought unbeatable. It was also a set-piece battle similar to the kind that had been fought in the latter stages of the First World War, with soldiers advancing under a heavy barrage and battalions leap-frogging forward to take their objectives. For the attack of the 51st (Highland) Division the intention was to secure 7,000 yards of desert fighting across minefields and barbed wire, with the division advancing in six channels towards their objectives. For the 7th battalion C Company had the objectives Paisley and Renfrew and Mons Meg (Red Line) while D Company was ordered to take Renfrew and Halkirk (Green Line) before moving on Greenock (Red Line). The plan was that the other two companies would then leapfrog them. At 21.40 a huge artillery barrage opened up as hundreds of guns fired towards the German lines and the Scots swept into the attack 20 minutes later. According to the battalion War Diary the first 100 yards were covered in three minutes.

Although there were problems in getting the armoured support and there were heavy casualties in A and D Companies all the first objectives were quickly taken with the follow-up forces passing through the first wave. By dawn the following day the second objectives had also been taken and the battle moved into its next phase, which Montgomery promised would be a 'dog-fight'. All the time shelling continued on either side and tank battles raged as British Sherman tanks engaged the enemy lines. The battle continued for over a week and every Highlander experienced the common lot of the 51st (Highland) Division – of being under constant mortar- and shell-fire and of being pinned down by artillery as the forward formations attempted to make the final breakthrough. However, the speed and aggression of the Allied assault had broken the enemy's will to resist and on 3 November came the joyous confirmation from the BBC that there had been 'a great victory in North Africa'. That same day Operation Supercharge was put into effect as British, Indian and New Zealand forces fought their way out of the German lines of barbed wire and minefields to allow the armoured forces to begin the chase after the now retreating German and Italian armies. Soon Montgomery's advancing men were passing well-known names which had become familiar to the Allies during the years of attack and retreat – Benghazi, Sidi Barrani, El Agheila, El Adem, Mersa Brega – as they raced towards the strategically important goal of the port of Tripoli, which fell at the end of January 1943.

The next stage was the advance to Tunis to link up with the First Army, which was approaching to rendezvous with the Eighth Army. (A joint British and US army had landed in Morocco and Algiers at the beginning of November 1942, as part of Operation Torch.) Amongst those serving in the 78th Division was 8th Argylls, which had landed in Algiers as part of the reinforcements. Also in the force was the old 6th battalion, now 93rd Anti-Tank Regiment RA, which provided V Corps with anti-tank support. Both formations saw considerable action in the fighting to take Tunis but by then the end was in sight. On 6 April Montgomery's forces had broken through at Wadi Akarit, having breached the Mareth Line a month earlier, and the coastal route to Tunis was open. With the two armies converging on Tunis Axis resistance began to crumble – Rommel had already left the battle front, leaving General Hans-Jürgen von Arnim in command – and amidst chaotic conditions the Germans capitulated on 12 May. The fighting in North Africa had finally come to an end.

NINE

The Second World War: 1943–45

The British victory at El Alamein was a turning point in the war. Not only were the church bells rung throughout the country to celebrate the Eighth Army's victory, but Montgomery had proved that the British soldier had nothing to fear in action against an enemy which had been thought to be unbeatable. Even so, it was only an interlude, if a welcome one. Giving a bloody nose to Rommel's Afrika Korps had provided a marvellous fillip for morale both within and outwith the armed forces, but it was not the end of the war. Ahead lay almost three years of hard fighting and there was still much to do – in addition to dealing with the Japanese in the Pacific and in Burma the Allies faced a determined and ruthless enemy in Europe, where the brunt of the fighting was being borne by the Red Army in the heartlands of the Soviet Union. In the short term, for the British and US forces, the next stage of the war involved the capture of Sicily as a precursor to the invasion of Italy, a move which would lead to the final securing of the Mediterranean, with its vital maritime routes to India and the Far East.

The Sicilian operation had been planned before final victory in North Africa: it called for a British seaborne assault by Montgomery's Eighth Army between Syracuse and the Pachino peninsula on the island's south-eastern coast, while the US I and II Armored Corps under the command of General George Smith Patton would land on a 40-mile front along the southern coast between Gela and Scoglitti, and Licata on the left flank. There would also be an airborne assault carried out by the US 82nd Airborne Division and the British 1st Airborne Division to attack targets in the inland area and to secure the landing grounds. Once ashore Montgomery planned to create a bridgehead and to make safe the ports of Syracuse and Licata before moving rapidly north to take Messina while Patton's forces covered the left flank.

SICILY

1st, 7th and 8th battalions

First ashore in 154 Brigade was 7th Argylls, which landed unopposed at Portopalo in the early hours of 10 July. The brigade's initial task was to form a bridgehead before marching northwards, and first contact with the enemy was made at Bucheri before pushing into the Plain of Catania. The next target was the airfield at Gerbini, which was duly attacked on the night of 20 July. Two days earlier the brigade had passed through the Stimpato bridgehead and had moved quickly towards the Simeto River. The omens looked good but the advance ground to a halt at Sferro, more than a mile from the air base which was defended by the elite Hermann Goering Division. Supported by artillery fire and backed by two squadrons of tanks, the 7th battalion went into the attack with C and D Companies in the lead. As had been expected, there was determined German resistance as the defenders had been alerted by the failure of an airborne operation in the previous week. Although all three battalions in the brigade managed to fight their way into the station and barrack areas of Sferro, the Germans regrouped and in the counter-attack 7th Argylls lost 18 officers, including the commanding officer, and 160 soldiers killed and wounded. In his diary Montgomery blamed the setback on the strength of the German resistance – 'he kept dropping small parties of very stout-hearted parachute troops in order to stiffen up his weak places' – but the failure to take the airfield was a serious blow which forced the British commander to rethink his tactics. Instead of forcing the issue on the Plain of Catania he decided to make a flank attack to the west of Mount Etna and to call up his reserves, including the 78th Division, which included 8th Argylls.

On its arrival towards the end of July the new division operated on the right of the Canadian forces to take ground vacated by the 51st (Highland) Division. During the attack on Catenanuova there was a stroke of luck when a German officer was captured while carrying detailed plans for the German defence of Sicily and the eventual withdrawal from the island. For the 8th battalion the next objective was the fortress town of Centuripe – known to every soldier in the division as 'Cherry Ripe' – which sat on a high outcrop between the valleys of the Rivers Dittaino and Simeto and could only be approached by a narrow road with steep hairpin bends. To make matters worse, the surrounding area had been heavily mined and the German defenders included elite parachute and SS troops. The battle for Centuripe began in the early hours of 1 August and it soon proved to be a bloody business. To 36th Brigade fell the task of capturing a position on the ridge so that an attack could be made at first light, but the Germans were well dug in and prepared to counter the British move. When 8th Argylls arrived at the first objective on the ridge the Germans held their fire until the leading X and R Companies were in the open before firing their machine guns. Within 48 hours the battalion had been fought to a standstill and had taken heavy casualties. It took time for it to be relieved and all three brigades in the division were involved in the final rounds of the battle, which saw fierce close-quarter combat in the narrow cobbled streets. Quite rightly, Montgomery called the capture of Centuripe 'a wonderful feat of arms'.

In the aftermath 8th Argylls was involved in the capture of Adrano, but the delays had stymied Montgomery's plan to push rapidly up the eastern side of Sicily – Patton had made better progress on the left – and it was not until 2 August that the Allies were in a position to move jointly on Messina. By then the German and Italian high command had decided that the island was indefensible and put into action the detailed plans for evacuation which began on 11 August. Sicily fell on 16 August, but some of the gloss was taken off the victory when over 100,000 German and Italian soldiers plus 9,800 vehicles were evacuated across the Straits of Messina to fight again in Italy. In October, 7th Argylls returned to Britain with 51st (Highland) Division for the next operation, the invasion of France, while the 8th battalion moved to Italy with 78th Division, landing at Taranto on 25 September.

Mention must also be made of the 1st battalion, which re-entered the fray after its peregrinations in the Middle East and Eritrea. During the landing operations it was employed as the infantry component of a 'Beach Brick' (33rd Beach Group), an all-arms support unit created to hold and maintain a beach-head to enable stores and ammunition to be unloaded. In the 1st battalion's case its main responsibility was to provide backing for the 5th Division during its landing on the right flank south of Syracuse. One of the Argyll officers working on the beaches was lucky to be there at all. Major Malcolm McAlister-Hall, a pre-war regular, was one of those who had been left behind on Crete and had been taken into German captivity in Athens. He and three others had made good their escape by the simple expedient of hiding behind loaves of bread in the cookhouse and waiting for darkness before slipping away. Once free, McAlister-Hall succeeded in making his way to Turkey, where British consular officials gave him a false identity as a Jewish refugee bound for Palestine. Eventually he got back to his battalion in Eritrea and was awarded the Military Cross. Unfortunately, while serving as a beach brick officer in Sicily he stepped on a mine and badly wounded his leg. On recuperating he joined the 7th battalion during the fighting in north-west Europe in 1945 (see below).

ITALY

1st, 6th (93rd Anti-Tank Regiment RA) and 8th battalions

Following the decisive victories in North Africa and the capture of Sicily in the summer of 1943 Italy had been invaded by the British and US allies in September. The US Fifth Army (General Mark Clark) landed with a British corps at Salerno on 9 September, while the British Eighth Army had arrived a few days earlier, having crossed the Straits of Messina and landed at Reggio. At the same time the Italians had surrendered, but while the Allies dithered over acceptance of the terms the Germans moved 16 divisions into Italy to continue the war and these forces were to prove more than a handful for the Allies. Although the landings at Salerno had been strongly opposed the Allied armies had moved north from Naples, where they met fierce resistance along a defensive position known as the Gustav Line. On arrival in Italy 8th Argylls moved north to Termoli on the Adriatic coast, where commando forces had been landed to engage the German defenders. The battalion's first task was very similar to the one undertaken at Centuripe – to capture the precipitous village of San Giacomo, which lay some miles inland. The attack began on 4 October with B Company in the lead, but as had happened in similar circumstances in Sicily the Germans were well dug in and produced heavy machine-gun and mortar fire which prevented further progress even when X and R Companies were committed to the battle. It soon became clear that the Germans were occupying San Giacomo in greater strength than the Argylls had anticipated and the commanding officer, Lieutenant-Colonel A.W. Scott-Elliot, was forced to give the order to withdraw. During the fighting the battalion lost 162 casualties killed and wounded. Amongst the dead was Major Jack Anderson, who had been awarded the Victoria Cross in Tunisia six months earlier (see Appendix).

Following its deployment as a 'Beach Brick' in Sicily the 1st battalion repeated the task with 33rd Beach Group for the invasion of southern Italy, but on completion of the task it returned to internal security duties in Egypt, where it was subjected to a good deal of turbulence as far as personnel were concerned. In December 1943 123 soldiers in the higher medical categories were transferred to the 2nd Highland Light Infantry for training as mountain troops, and these were replaced by a draft of recruits from Queen's Own Cameron Highlanders. The one highlight was being given responsibility for providing security at the Mena House conference at the end of November, when Churchill met the US president, Franklin D. Roosevelt, ahead of the subsequent 'Big Three' summit in Tehran with Stalin. All uncertainty about the future came to an end in February 1944, when the battalion was ordered to embark for Taranto to join 19 Indian Infantry Brigade in the 8th Indian Division. As the regimental historian makes clear, it was to be a happy and fateful association:

Under the sign [divisional badge] of the 'three wee floo-ers' [a yellow four-leafed clover flanked by two three-leafed clovers] the Battalion fought its way through snow and rainstorm, heat and mud, to the final victory in the fertile valley of the River Po.

THE SECOND WORLD WAR: 1943–45

    Across the rivers Garigliano, Melfa, Liri, Arno, Senio and Po, over the towering peaks of the Apennines, through the fruit orchards and cornfields of the Po valley the war graves bear witness to the passage of the Battalion. The spirit of comradeship and mutual admiration which grew up between the Indian fighting man and his British counterpart in the 8th Indian Division was one of the reasons why the name of '8th Indian' was feared and respected even amongst the German paratroopers.

In short, that was the experience of 1st Argylls from the moment it joined its new division in the little village of Castel Frentano to the final stages of the fighting near Rovigo 15 months later, and in that period the battalion saw some of the fiercest fighting of the Italian campaign. By the time that 1st Argylls arrived in Italy the Germans had consolidated their defences along the Gustav Line with the result that offensives were confined to the coastal flanks. In the centre the mountainous terrain and obstacles such as the rivers Garigliano and Liri made any advance difficult and hopes for an early breakthrough quickly faded. To break the impasse it was decided to mount an amphibious operation which would land Allied forces behind the German defensive positions at Anzio, but due to Allied dithering and German resolve the landings faltered for several weeks. This was a grim period for the Allies as the push towards Rome had also been held up in the Liri Valley due to the German occupation of the monastery at Monte Cassino, the home of the Benedictine Order. It stood on high ground outside the town of the same name, which had been razed to the ground, and, being partially occupied by German forces, became the scene of fierce fighting. The stalemate was broken in mid-May when Cassino finally fell, opening the Liri Valley route, and at the same time US VI Corps managed to break out of the Anzio bridgehead.

During the Cassino operations the 1st battalion was given the task of securing a position known as the San Angelo 'Horseshoe' with 17 and 19 Brigades, while the 8th battalion was held in reserve with 78th Division to exploit the situation as the battle developed. Before going into the attack the brigades had to cross the River Rapido, a tributary of the Liri, on 11 May, but there were difficulties when the Germans put down smoke and the 1st battalion was pinned down on the opposite bank before tanks were sent to allow the men to retire. During the crossing the battalion lost two officers and 12 soldiers killed and three officers and 57 soldiers wounded. The 'horseshoe' objective was finally taken on 16 May. The road to Rome was now open and between 28 May and 4 June the advance did not falter. Ahead lay the Allied move across the River Arno into the mountainous areas to the north as the enemy grimly held on to its defensive positions along the Gothic Line which stretched from Carrara in the west to Pesaro on the Adriatic. Delaying actions by the Germans held up progress and it did not help that both the British and the US armies were being denuded to reinforce the operations in France and north-west Europe following the success of the invasion of Normandy earlier in the summer (see below). The weather, too, worsened and as September gave way to October and November the battalion found itself fighting over some of the worst terrain experienced by British soldiers during the war in Europe. As the 1st battalion's war historian noted, it was an environment which any soldier of the Second World War would have recognised:

> The Battalion was beginning to get used, as the British soldier can get used to anything, to that detached and exclusive world of the infantry – and those who work with them – know; a world which presents a standard appearance of shell-holes, or burnt-out vehicles, charred,

rusty and hideous, of sheaves of telephone cables criss-crossing the ditches and hedgerows; of warning notice boards which state 'Road under shell-fire'; of blasted trees and shattered houses; of wayside graves and of a peculiar all-pervading smell.

The final effort took both Argyll battalions through the fighting at Monte Arbertino, Cavallara and Cerere onwards to the River Senio and the final defeat of the German army in northern Italy. In November 1943 the 6th battalion had also arrived in Italy to provide anti-tank support for V Corps in the pursuit beyond the Gothic Line towards the River Santerno. Finally, at the end of April in Ferrara the pipes and drums of 1st and 8th Argylls combined to beat Retreat to the 'open-mouthed astonishment and roars of applause' of the medieval city's inhabitants. A few days later came the news of the unconditional surrender of all German forces in Italy.

FRANCE AND NORTH-WEST EUROPE
2nd (new), 5th (91st Anti-Tank Regiment RA), 7th and 9th battalions (54th Light Anti-Aircraft Regiment RA)

From the outset of US involvement in the Second World War their military planners had made a strong case for an early attack on the European mainland. In fact the decision to press ahead with the invasion of north-west Europe had been taken as early as May 1943 at an Allied conference in Washington, and planning for it began under joint US–British direction immediately after the summit had ended. The main desiderata for the cross-Channel amphibious attack were quickly established: a landing area with shallow beaches and without obstacles which was within range of Allied air power, the neutralisation of local defences to allow a build-up which would equal the strength of the German defenders and the presence of a large port for reinforcement and re-supply.

Deception also formed part of the plan: the idea was to persuade the Germans that the assault would be made across the narrowest part of the English Channel at Pas de Calais, where the beaches were shallow and led into the hinterland without the obstacles of cliffs and high ground. It also offered the opportunity to make a quick strike into the Low Countries and from there into Germany. All those reasons made Pas de Calais the ideal place for invasion, but because it was the obvious location it was quickly discounted as the Allied planners realised that their German counterparts would deploy the bulk of their defensive forces there. By the end of the summer the plan was shown to the Allied leadership at the Quadrant conference in Quebec. The chosen landing ground was the Baie de la Seine in Normandy, between Le Havre and the Cotentin peninsula, an area which met all the criteria, including a deepwater port at Cherbourg.

The initial planning called for an invasion force of three divisions plus airborne forces which would create a bridgehead through which reinforcements could be landed quickly to break out into Normandy and Brittany. Success would depend on the ability of the Allies to build up forces more rapidly than the Germans could find reinforcements. With that in mind, it was essential to deny the enemy by destroying road and rail communications in northern France. Although Montgomery agreed with the main principles of the plan, he put forward an alternative proposal to attack in greater weight along a broader front and with a larger airborne contribution. This was backed by Eisenhower, who activated his headquarters – Supreme Headquarters Allied Expeditionary Force (SHAEF) – in February. It was agreed that the initial assault should be made by five divisions, two US, two British and one Canadian, with one British and two US airborne divisions operating on the flanks. The D-Day invasion began on 6 June with the airborne forces securing the flanks overnight while the main assault went in at dawn, preceded by a mighty bombardment from 2,000 warships in the Channel. By the end of the day the assault divisions were ashore and the five landing areas – Utah, Omaha, Gold, Sword and Juno – had been secured with the loss of fewer than 10,000 casualties (killed, wounded or missing), fewer than expected.

Both of the Argyll infantry battalions took part in the fighting in Normandy following the D–Day landings. The first in action was the 7th battalion on 14 June, when 154 Brigade went into the attack under the operational command of 6th Airborne Division to defend the vital Orne bridges. The battalion's position on the Bois de Bavent ridge was heavily wooded and interspersed with orchards and small fields divided by thick hedges – difficult ground for infantrymen to hold. During the night of 24 June heavy enemy bombing forced the battalion to take cover in slit trenches and the battalion used its carriers to take ammunition to 7th Black Watch in the forward positions. Unfortunately, the constant enemy activity and the failure to break out of the Caen perimeter had a debilitating effect on the 51st (Highland) Division. Having proved itself in North Africa as one of the finest fighting formations in the British Army, it lost its cutting edge in Normandy and according to the corps commander, Lieutenant-General Sir Brian Horrocks, 'during the Normandy fighting they were not at their best'. (A similar malaise afflicted 7th Armoured Division.) So serious was the fall in morale that in mid-July Montgomery reported to the Chief of the Imperial General Staff that the 51st (Highland) Division was no longer 'battleworthy' and 'does not fight with determination'. Some idea of the widespread unrest can be found in the recollections of Captain Ian Cameron, 7th Argylls, which were published in the divisional history:

> Not a day passed without the battalion area being subjected
> to heavy shelling and mortaring and although our casualties

were not heavy, there was a continual drain on personnel. In former campaigns the 51st Division had always been used aggressively and wherever there was an attack HD always took part in it. This was the first time that the battalion had to sit for lengthy periods in a defensive position without launching an attack, and this became very monotonous.

Another officer admitted that 'any orders that involved life-threatening activity were ignored or watered down, especially if given by young officers without battle training.' As a result of this general slump in morale, which could have been disastrous for every regiment in the division, Montgomery was forced to sack its commander, Wimberley's successor, Major-General Charles Bullen-Smith MC, late King's Own Scottish Borderers, on the grounds that 'the men won't fight for you'. It was a drastic move to make in the middle of a battle that had not yet been won, but although Montgomery was loath to make it he had no option. Bullen-Smith was replaced by Major-General T.G. Rennie, a former commanding officer of 5th Black Watch who had been commanding the 3rd Infantry Division, the famous 'Ironsides'.

At the same time the 51st (Highland) Division was taken out of the line for a short period of rest and recuperation at Cazelle, north-west of Caen, and some of the under-strength battalions, including 7th Argylls, were reinforced with fresh soldiers, many of them from English regiments. The tonic seemed to work and soon company commanders were able to report that their men were returning to the form which had made the division such a success in North Africa and Sicily. They needed to be on top of their game, for ahead lay Operation Totalise, a thrust out of Caen towards Falaise mounted by the Canadian First Army with 51st (Highland) Division in support. Before the attack began, on 8 August, Rennie reminded his senior officers that it could be 'the decisive battle in France' and that he expected every soldier in the division to show the same 'determination and offensive spirit' that they had demonstrated at Alamein. Although the Germans put up stout resistance Falaise fell on 16 August and the way to the River Seine was open.

At the time of the breakout 2nd Argylls had arrived in France as part of 15th (Scottish) Division, which landed towards the end of June. The attacking forces immediately found themselves involved in heavy fighting against German positions on the Eterville Ridge south of Odon as part of Operation Epsom. During the operations the 2nd battalion was brigaded with 10th Highland Light Infantry and 2nd Gordon Highlanders: the latter battalion was an ideal companion for 2nd Argylls as it, too, had been re-formed from a Territorial battalion after the regular 2nd Gordons had been forced to surrender at Singapore. The operation began on 26 June in poor weather conditions with heavy rain, which meant that there would only be limited air cover. When the brigade went into the attack a hailstorm began and the drizzle continued throughout the day as 15th (Scottish) Division pushed towards the small town of Cheux. Armoured support was provided by 11th Armoured Division and 31st Tank Brigade, but the presence of the tanks was often a mixed blessing as they attracted heavy German defensive fire and added to the confusion, one watching staff officer noting that 'what little space was left in the lanes seemed to be filled by our own tanks, closed down and deaf to all appeals. None who was in Cheux that morning is likely to forget the confusion.' During the fighting 2nd Argylls pushed forward with great rapidity and élan to create a bridgehead at Tourmauville, in so doing braving intensive German machine-gun fire but 'with miraculously few casualties'. The next objective was Gavrus, where the bridges were undefended, but as the battalion's war historian revealed, it took five hours to travel a mile:

It [2nd Argylls] set off at once through the thick woods lining both banks of the Odon. All-round defence in such country was impossible. The going was vile, and at one place the whole march was held up for over an hour while the anti-tank guns were manhandled over a sticky patch. Any well-planned ambush might have proved fatal; but fortunately there were only a few false alarms of snipers and the Battalion arrived intact and complete at the Gavrus bridgehead before dark.

It was the calm before the storm. Ahead lay 48 hours of fierce fighting against German armour and infantry as 2nd Argylls bore the brunt of the enemy's counter-attack. To meet the Allied invasion Hitler had ordered II SS Panzer Corps to move from Poland, and it was the 2nd battalion's fate to meet the first blows from these battle-hardened veterans equipped with Panther and Mark IV main battle tanks. The battle continued for a week before the division was withdrawn without achieving the expected breakthrough but other objectives had been gained in return for the 2,500 casualties killed and wounded. Although Operation Epsom was not counted as a complete tactical success, it had taken the sting out of the German counter-attack and in so doing had prevented German armour from driving a wedge between the Allied forces as they fought their way south through what became known as the 'Scottish Corridor'. As John Keegan put it in his history of the campaign in Normandy, the 2nd battalion's battling performance at Gavrus exemplified the tenacity of the resistance offered by the men and 'stood fit to rank with those other small epics of Argyll and Scottish stubbornness, the destruction of the 93rd at the battle of New Orleans and the stand of the 'thin red line' at Balaclava [sic].'

The next problem for the Allies was overstretch – as the attacking forces moved away from the beach-heads their supply lines became longer and that had an impact on the speed of their advance into north-west Europe. It also meant that the war would not end in 1944. In September the Highland Division took part in the operations to capture the ports of Le Havre and Dunkirk, but this was preceded by a highly emotional moment when St Valéry was retaken amidst scenes of great local jubilation. Each brigade in the division was placed in roughly the same position that had been occupied by their predecessors in 1940 and that evening (3 September) the massed pipes and drums played Retreat outside the divisional headquarters at Cailleville. From there the advance took the division into Flanders and on into Holland where the flat 'polder' lowlands had been flooded, causing inevitable problems. This included a period of intensive fighting as both the 15th (Scottish) Division and the 51st (Highland) Division fought their way over a succession of formidable water obstacles towards the River Maas. For everyone in both Argyll battalions the flooded and frozen landscape was 'an abomination of desolation', with hard going in the increasingly wet winter weather conditions.

In an attempt to break the German defensive positions along the border with Holland the Allies launched Operation Veritable on 8 February. For the 2nd battalion this involved fighting at Cleve to the north while the 7th battalion took part in the 51st (Highland) Division's offensive in the southern Reichswald. However, despite the atrocious weather conditions and the strength of the German resistance the division ended Operation Veritable on a high note, taking the town of Goch in some of the fiercest fighting of the campaign. There was also some time to relax: at Tilburg the pipes and drums of 2nd and 7th Argylls combined to beat Retreat in the main square. Before engaging in Operation Veritable the division had ended 1944 by fighting in the Ardennes to help stem a fierce German counter-attack which created a dangerous salient or 'bulge' in the Allied lines, hence the action's alternative name, the

Battle of the Bulge. Fighting in support of the US Ninth Army in the Ourthe Valley, 7th Argylls lost 38 casualties during the capture of key points at Lavaux, Beaulieu and Cens.

Ahead lay the Rhine crossing and the break-in to the industrial areas of the Ruhr which would decide the final course of the war. By then it was not so much a question of *if* the Germans could be defeated but *when* they would be defeated. For the potentially dangerous and difficult task of attacking across the Rhine Montgomery chose the 15th (Scottish) Division and 51st (Highland) Division, using Buffalo amphibious vehicles during the operation, which began on the night of 24 March. (Other innovative armoured fighting vehicles introduced at this time included Kangaroos, specially adapted Sherman tanks with their gun turrets removed and capable of carrying a section of men.) For the 7th battalion this meant crossing the river at Rees, north-west of Wessel, and for the battalion's historian 'it was a thrilling moment when these great clumsy vehicles lumbered into the water and started swimming across to the far bank.' During the crossing by the 2nd battalion the Buffalos of D Company encountered problems landing and as a result the battalion was split up during the subsequent fighting at the village of Hübsch, which was held by German paratroopers. There was better luck for the 7th battalion, which landed relatively unopposed; the moment was described in the divisional history by the adjutant, Captain Angus Stewart:

> At 8pm we got into our Buffaloes, ponderous, clumsy creatures looking like the original tanks of 1916. About 8 feet high on dry land, driven both on land and water by great tracks which travel round the whole perimeter of the vehicle instead of on bogies as on a modern tank. They carry a platoon of men or a small vehicle like a jeep or carrier. At nine o'clock the Argylls entered the water and

chugged across, none failed, none sank, all landed our men where we wanted them.

Once on the other side the battalion was involved in heavy fighting to take the village of Bienen, as the opposition offered intensive resistance. In the aftermath of the crossing the 51st (Highland) Division suffered a tragedy when General Rennie was killed during a heavy German mortar attack near the town of Rees. It was a shattering blow, as Rennie had been a popular and inspiring commander. He was succeeded by Major-General (later Lieutenant-General Sir) Gordon MacMillan, an experienced and well-liked commander and the senior Argyll and Sutherland Highlander of the Second World War. The Rhine crossing was the beginning of the end, and for the next month the 51st (Highland) Division was constantly on the move as it fought its way north towards Bremen and Bremerhaven, which was reached on 8 May. At the same time 15th (Scottish) Division reached Gros Hansdorf to the north-east of Hamburg, having completed the crossing of the River Elbe at Artlenburg on 30 April when it sustained its last casualties of the war from enemy gunfire and aerial bombardment. In one incident 50 soldiers were killed or wounded while the battalion was assembling in a quarry. With the war almost over it was a cruel blow for the regiment to sustain.

Also taking part in the post-D-Day operations and the advance into Germany was the 5th battalion, operating as 91st Anti-Tank Regiment RA, which provided the anti-tank support for VIII Corps (Lieutenant-General Sir Richard O'Connor) consisting of 11th (Armoured) Division, 15th (Scottish) Division and 43rd (Wessex) Division, and its experiences were broadly similar to those of the 2nd and 7th Argylls. As the corps anti-tank specialists, the regiment was obliged to provide the main firepower to take on the formidable German armoured opposition, which included Tiger tanks with their powerful 88mm guns. Like every other soldier in the British Army the men of 91ˢᵗ Anti-Tank regiment had their share of the dangers and demands of war, as their historian, Desmond Flower, found in October when he witnessed an attack at Overloorn and Venraij, where 114 battery supported 15ᵗʰ (Scottish) while 146 battery was placed under the command of 3ʳᵈ Division:

> It was a bloody day's fighting. The infantry, making a silent crossing in the early morning, was forced to advance straight across the open fields. The armour's efforts were completely abortive. The Churchills sent down to the Molenbeek to fill the dykes with faggots bogged down before they reached their destination, were shot up, or found their task impossible when they got there. The tanks therefore pushed round into the woods on to the right, where they were shelled and mortared for hours on end, while a recce party went forward on foot in the hope of finding some way over the obstacle. Everywhere the fair green turf was a delusion, for as soon as anything heavier than a man attempted to traverse it, it gave way. The 2 Lincolns, for example, lost seventy killed in one small field when they were observed. To make the scene more horrible, the Churchills working down to the dyke to attempt bridging operations were forced by the narrowness of the track to drive over the bodies of their fallen comrades.

In October 1944 there was a potentially damaging change when the 91ˢᵗ Anti-Tank Regiment was replaced in VIII Corps by the 63ʳᵈ Anti-Tank Regiment (Queen's Own Oxfordshire Hussars Yeomanry), which had been trained to serve in the 61ˢᵗ Division but had failed to see action. Due to internal army politics it was earmarked to replace the Argyll gunners, but as it had no experience of operating the M-10 it was decided to replace two of its batteries with 144 and 146 batteries from 91st Anti-Tank Regiment. In return the 63rd sent over two of its batteries and the break-up of the two regiments turned out to be a sorry business which was bad for both of them – the Oxfordshire Hussars were a distinguished yeomanry regiment in which Churchill had once served and the 91st had inherited the ethos and fighting spirit of 5th Argylls. In its new guise the revamped 5th battalion took part in the fighting for the Reichswald and the operations from the Rhine to the Elbe. Following its escape at Dunkirk, 54th Light Anti-Aircraft Regiment (formerly 9th battalion) spent most of the pre-D-Day period protecting airfields in England, but in May 1943 it had the satisfaction of being allowed to wear the tam o'shanter with Argyll cap badge. At the same time, permission was given to collect the pipes and drums from Dumbarton Castle, a move which allowed the gunners to re-forge their links with the old 9th battalion. Although 54th LAA Regiment did not take part in the D-Day landings it ended the war in north-west Europe serving with the Canadian First Army.

The German capitulation was followed by Victory in Europe (VE) Day, which was celebrated on 8 May, and four days later the Highland Division mounted a victory parade in Bremerhaven with the salute being taken by Lieutenant-General Sir Brian Horrocks, commander of XXX Corps. 'As they marched past the General, the sound of the pipes just seemed to lift you, and we cheered our heads off,' recalled one onlooker. 'One by one the regiments passed us, and it was a blaze of colour with all the different regimental tartans on display.' Ahead lay the task of pacifying and occupying Germany and beginning the job of rebuilding the shattered country. The end of the war also saw the demise of the Argylls' Territorial infantry battalions (7th and 8th) as well as the disbandment of the three battalions which had served as regiments of the Royal Artillery (5th,

6th and 9th). Before ending its service overseas the 8th battalion was part of the occupation force in Austria, where it was involved in the controversial decision to hand over to the Red Army Cossack soldiers who had served in SS divisions. Although this was a political decision which had been decided by the Allied powers at an earlier summit meeting in Yalta it was an unpleasant task for the British soldiers involved in the operation, as the Cossacks were being sent to a certain death.

TEN

Korea, Crater and the Cold War

Britain ended the Second World War on the victorious side – with her allies she had extirpated the evil of Nazi ideology and put paid to Japanese imperialist ambitions in the Far East – but the war had been won at a high cost. Fighting it had drained Britain financially, and Clement Attlee's post-war Labour government found itself having to grapple with the problems of recession, shortages and financial restrictions imposed by the shattered economy. The war had cost the country £3,000 million, exports had fallen below pre-war levels and loans from the US had weakened the value of sterling. Many of the heavy industries, including coal-mining, were not productive or competitive, and transport and communications were suffering from a lack of planning and investment. Rationing remained in being until 1954 and the poor standing of the economy had a knock-on effect on the armed forces where cutbacks and scaling-down were the order of the day. By 1951 the size of the infantry had shrunk to 20 per cent of the army's total size – 88,100 soldiers out of a total strength of 417,800, all line infantry regiments had been reduced to a single battalion and the combat units had fallen to 184, consisting of 77 infantry battalions, eight Gurkha battalions, 69 artillery regiments and 30 armoured regiments. The specialist corps – the Royal Engineers, the Royal Electrical and Mechanical Engineers, the Royal Army Service Corps, the Royal Army Ordnance Corps – had all expanded during the war and would remain dominant in peacetime. As evidence of that shift towards harnessing modern technology, in 1949 those corps employed more lieutenant-colonels on their complement than the whole of the infantry put together.

There was also a need to garrison Germany, first as an army of occupation and then with the creation of the British Army of the Rhine (BAOR), which came into being in 1949 as Britain's contribution to the North Atlantic Treaty Organisation (NATO) and the Northern Army Group in Germany (plus Norway and Denmark) came under the command of British generals. This was Britain's contribution to the post-war defence of western Europe and in some respects Germany came to be regarded, somewhat tenuously, as the army's successor to India, ideal for training. However, even the most enthusiastic promoters of that theory had to admit that the country lacked the conditions, the climate and, it has to be said, the mystique. During BAOR's early years the rationale for being in post-war Germany, by then divided into West and East, was not always apparent to soldiers, but following the blockade of Berlin in 1948 the confrontation between NATO and the Soviet Union became increasingly bitter and belligerent. Later, the period would be known as the Cold War and for the rest of the century West Germany was to be a second home for The Argyll and Sutherland Highlanders and the British Army.

During the immediate post-war years, in common with the rest of the infantry the regiment underwent a dramatic decrease in size. For a start, the Territorial battalions were disbanded, albeit temporarily, as part of the process of demobilisation. Both the 7th and 8th battalions were restored in 1947 and remained in being until 1967, the latter having amalgamated with the 11th battalion, and the wartime artillery battalions continued in similar guises. There was a different fate for the two Regular battalions. The 1st battalion returned to Britain in 1945 before taking part in an arduous tour of internal security duties in Palestine at a time when tensions were running high between the Arab and Jewish populations as they struggled to gain the ascendancy. It was a deployment which Britain was hard-pressed to make and throughout the period the military units involved in internal security duties were severely overstretched.

Inevitably, fighting an invisible enemy had a demoralising effect on the members of the British security forces. They were able to disrupt terrorist activities and in some cases forestall them, as they did during Operation Elephant in March 1947 when martial law was declared for three weeks in Tel Aviv, Petach Tikva and Ramat Gan, but all too often the men of the 1st battalion found themselves reacting to situations about which they had no prior knowledge. This bred a siege mentality best expressed by the military historian Correlli Barnett, who served as a National Service conscript in Palestine in 1946: 'two British divisions and support troops, some 60,000 soldiers, were stuck in Palestine adding to the balance of payments deficit, carrying out clumsy and ineffective sweeps against the Jewish terrorists who were murdering their comrades, and otherwise doing nothing but guard their own barbed wire.' During the deployment the 1st battalion was brigaded with 2nd Oxfordshire and Buckinghamshire Light Infantry and 1st Royal Ulster Rifles in 6 Air Landing Brigade. Inevitably there were casualties: four killed in action, 10 wounded and five dead as a result of accidents.

During the same period the 2nd battalion had remained in Germany as part of the army of occupation until 1947. Its days were already numbered. In common with the other line infantry regiments of the British army, The Argyll and Sutherland Highlanders was forced to reduce its size to one battalion through the amalgamation of its 1st and 2nd battalions, with the latter being placed 'in suspended animation' to allow its customs and traditions to be preserved in the new 1st battalion. To commemorate the passing of the ways an amalgamation parade was held at Colchester on 30 October 1948 under the command of Lieutenant-Colonel E.A.F. Macpherson. Amongst the traditions and customs of the old 93rd the guard-mounting procedure was continued in the new 1st battalion, the march past 'Highland Laddie' is played before 'The Campbells are Coming' and the motto 'Sans Peur' became the battalion's war cry.

After beginning its life at Sobroan Barracks, Colchester, the new battalion left for Hong Kong in June 1949 and after a lengthy voyage quickly settled into its new home at Stanley Barracks on the south coast of the Crown Colony. The battalion formed 27 Brigade with 1st Middlesex Regiment and 1st Royal Leicestershire Regiment. It was a time of heightened tensions due to the unstable situation in neighbouring China, where the nationalist army under generalissimo Chiang Kai-Shek was being driven back by the increasingly dominant Communist forces. With Communist agencies making incursions over the border, the battalion was trained in internal security duties in support of the Hong Kong Police. Under normal circumstances the Hong Kong posting should have been a stress-free occasion – the regimental journal shows that there was 'plenty of recreational training' – but all that came to an end in the summer of 1950, when the North Koreans crossed the 38th parallel to invade their neighbours to the south.

Korea had been annexed by Japan in 1910 and had remained a Japanese colony until 1945, when the country had been split into two halves along the 38th parallel, the north becoming a Communist autocracy and the south a hastily organised democracy. Although the United Nations (UN) entertained hopes that the two Koreas might be united in the future, the two regimes were antagonistic to each other and resented the artificially created barrier which divided them. Any idea that they might find an accommodation was shattered on 25 June 1950, when North Korean troops attacked across the border. Shocked by the abruptness of the invasion, the US successfully persuaded the UN to take action – the argument in favour of armed intervention was helped by the absence of the Soviet Union from the Security Council in protest at the UN's refusal to recognise Communist China. The US acted quickly: General Douglas MacArthur, commanding the US Army in the Far East, was despatched from Japan to appraise the situation and by the end of July the US had four divisions in South Korea. Although the US forces had command of the air and the sea, they were powerless to halt the North Korean attack and by the end of August the UN forces were desperately defending the Pusan perimeter, their last line of defence in the south-east of the country.

At that stage of the war the first British contribution to the UN forces had arrived, in the shape of 27 Brigade with two infantry battalions – 1st Middlesex and 1st Argyll and Sutherland Highlanders. Getting them there was a taxing business and both battalions had been hurriedly reinforced with volunteers from other regiments but according to the novelist Eric Linklater, who wrote the British official history of the campaign, what they lacked in numbers they made up for in enthusiasm and a reliance on age-old traditions:

> Neither the Middlesex nor the Argylls could muster more than three rifle companies and there was no military principle to justify the despatch of and committing to battle of two weak battalions that had neither their own necessary transport nor their proper supporting arms. It was the desperate plight of the Americans in the Pusan

bridgehead that had compelled their sudden embarkation and as military principles were overridden by moral need so were the difficulties of their strange campaign to be overcome by recruitment, as it seemed, from the regimental spirit to which they were heirs. In the months to come both the Middlesex and the Argylls – though nearly half of them were youngsters doing their national training – were to enhance the pride and reputation, not only of the Diehards and the 91st, but of all the Army.

Such was the urgency of the situation that the battalion was pitched more or less immediately into the fight when 27 Brigade took over responsibility for a section of the UN line along the Naktong river south-west of Taegu. At the same time MacArthur was drawing up plans to break out of the perimeter and the offensive opened on 21 September with 27 Brigade on the left flank of the US line. A range of hills was their first objective and 1st Argylls was given the task of capturing Hill 282 on the left end of the ridge. This was accomplished at dawn on 23 September, with B Company on the right and C Company on the left, but almost immediately the men came under sustained enemy fire and casualties started mounting. At nine o'clock Major Kenneth Muir, the battalion second-in-command, arrived with stretcher-bearers and stayed on to organise the defences. With no artillery support the situation was in danger of becoming hopeless and the Argylls' commanding officer, Lieutenant-Colonel Leslie Neilson, requested an air strike on the neighbouring Hill 388, which the North Koreans occupied. This came in at 12.15 p.m. but to the dismay of those watching, the three US Air Force Mustang fighter-bombers attacked B and C Companies first with napalm bombs and then with machine-gun fire. Recognition panels had been displayed and the aircraft circled the target three times before attacking, but still the US pilots pressed home their attack. Only five officers and

35 other ranks from the two companies made good their escape. It was not the end of the incident. Muir led a counter-attack to retake the burning hilltop and although it succeeded the position could not be held, as the Argylls lacked sufficient men and were rapidly running out of ammunition. Throughout the action Muir continued to encourage his men but he was mortally wounded while helping to man a 2-inch mortar. His last words were reported to be: 'The Gooks [North Koreans] will never drive the Argylls off this hill.' For his courage Muir was posthumously awarded the Victoria Cross and the US Distinguished Service Cross. During the action the battalion lost 17 killed and missing and 79 wounded.

The incident was a grim reminder of the problems of forming a unified UN command from scratch; it was also indicative of the indifferent air–ground liaison during that early stage of the war. In the aftermath the battalion was hurriedly reinforced, many of the new arrivals being National Servicemen. Through a succession of National Service Acts wartime legislation for conscription had been kept in place and between then and 1963 2.3 million men served as National Servicemen, the majority in the army. In its final form the period of conscription was two years, following two earlier periods of 12 and 18 months and like every other regiment in the British Army the Argylls benefited from the contribution made by men who were the first peacetime conscripts in British history. The British brigade was also reinforced with the addition of 3rd Royal Australian Regiment and in its final form served as 27 Commonwealth Brigade.

Following the breakout from the Pusan perimeter the UN forces pushed north towards Pyongyang, with the brigade acting as the spearhead for the US 1st Cavalry Division. During this phase the enemy resistance started faltering, but it soon became clear that the North Koreans were being reinforced by soldiers from the Chinese Army. Following an action at the Chongchon river the battalion started collecting its first evidence that the Chinese were involved in the war when they moved forward to inspect the enemy casualties. In his memoir Colin Mitchell, a future commanding officer but then a young lieutenant, remembered the moment when the discovery was made:

> They were unlike any enemy I had seen before. They wore thick padded clothing which made them look like little Michelin men. I turned one body over with my foot, and saw that he wore a peaked cap with a red star badge. These soldiers were Chinese. I then turned another over and, as I looked down at him, he opened one eye and looked up at me. I shot him with my Luger [pistol], shouting to the platoon, 'they're alive!' It was quickly over and all the enemy lay dead.

The arrival of the Chinese changed everything and once again the UN forces were forced to retire south across the 38th parallel. At the same time the bitter winter weather made conditions extremely difficult and the battalion was not unhappy when it was relieved in March 1951 and then shipped back to Hong Kong. During the eight months of almost continual fighting the Argylls had lost 35 killed and 136 wounded. A further nine were killed and 45 wounded amongst those who stayed on to reinforce other regiments, notably 1st King's Own Scottish Borderers. A year later 1st Argylls returned to Britain, where it became the resident battalion in Edinburgh, responsible for carrying out public duties. During the tour, on 26 June 1953, the regiment received new colours from the Colonel-in-Chief, Queen Elizabeth II, whose coronation had taken place three weeks earlier.

A few months later the battalion returned to active service when it was deployed to the South American colony of British

Guiana (later Guyana), where the People's Progressive Party (PPP) under Cheddi Jagan had won a general election in April, only to be dismissed by the British governor ten months later. During the summer the PPP organised a number of strikes – the colony's main exports were sugar and timber – and Jagan called for the redistribution of resources to help the plight of the local population, most of whom lived in sub-standard housing and were poorly paid. Civil rights and the constitution were suspended, a state of martial law was declared and troops were rushed in from the British garrison in Jamaica. To reinforce the police and the local Volunteer Forces the Argylls were despatched to the colony on board the aircraft carrier HMS *Implacable*. According to the British government the PPP had 'completely destroyed the confidence of the business community and moderate opinion', but there was also a strong suspicion that the steps had been taken at the request of the US State Department. (This was confirmed when the official papers from the incident were declassified in 1983.)

During its deployment the battalion was based at the capital, Georgetown, and at Atkinson Field, a former US air force base close to the Demerara River. Its role was to provide aid to the civil power by backing up police operations during a further outbreak of trouble in April 1954, following Jagan's arrest for violating restriction orders. Although there were further outbreaks of violence, these were sporadic and for the most part the deployment was not dissimilar to any other in a colonial station during the same period. There were opportunities for sport, a parade was held for the Queen's Birthday and many of the men married local girls. In October the battalion was relieved by 2nd Black Watch and then air-lifted to Trinidad for the voyage back to Britain on board the troopship *Dilwara*. Eighteen months later the garrison was reduced to one infantry company and the colony became independent in May 1966.

Following a winter spent in freezing conditions at Pinefield Camp, Elgin, the battalion moved to Berlin in February 1955, travelling by ferry from Harwich to the Hook of Holland and then onwards by train. Montgomery Barracks in the former German capital had been built for the Luftwaffe in the late 1930s and proved to be comfortable and well equipped. This was the battalion's first experience of soldiering in post-war Germany, where one of the duties was to provide guards for the Spandau prison, which housed six convicted former members of the Nazi hierarchy. In the summer of 1956 the battalion moved back to Britain to be based at Blenheim Barracks, Bury St Edmunds, where it joined 19 Brigade, the other battalions being 1st Royal Scots and 1st West Yorkshire Regiment, but already the international situation was becoming tense as a result of the seizure and nationalisation of the Suez Canal by the Egyptian leader, Colonel Gamul Abdul Nasser. In response, the battalion was brought up to war strength with the recall of 200 reservists and preparations were put in hand for the brigade to be deployed to the Mediterranean.

Following Nasser's proclamation the British prime minister, Anthony Eden, instructed the British chiefs of staff to prepare a plan to recapture the canal in conjunction with French forces, but nothing happened until November. The need to find a diplomatic solution and the questionable legality of any operation, plus deep divisions about the policy to be pursued, all combined to create a serious question mark over the enterprise and the outcome was perhaps predictable. The invasion was successfully launched and executed using airborne and commando forces and by 6 November all Egyptian resistance had come to an end but by then the 'war' was over before it had begun. Soviet belligerency and US financial pressure forced Eden to call a ceasefire and to turn the problem over to the UN. It was a humiliating order which Britain had no option but to accept as Washington had refused to support

Britain's application to the International Monetary Fund for a loan to support the falling pound unless those conditions were met.

While these events were taking place 1st Argylls was still at sea and there was a good deal of uncertainty about what would happen next. In the event, 19 Brigade began disembarking at Port Said on 13 November and took over the positions being held by 45 Commando, which had been one of the original invasion formations. Despite the ceasefire the battalion found itself virtually in a war zone. Port Said was the entrance to the Suez Canal and anti-British feelings were running high in the local population, especially in the area known as Arab Town. Weapons were freely available and the danger of attacks on patrols were as high as they had been in Cyprus. At the same time, British troops had to undertake humanitarian aid operations and to work in conjunction with UN forces after their deployment in mid-December. Predictably, it was a frustrating time for the men of the Argylls, who had left Britain prepared to take part in an offensive action but had ended up taking part in ill-defined peace-keeping operations knowing that their involvement had been roundly condemned by the rest of the world. By 23 December the ill-advised adventure was over when the last British troops left Port Said and, thanks to some efficient planning, the battalion managed to get back to Scotland for the New Year celebrations.

Bury St Edmunds was the Argylls' base until the beginning of 1958, when the battalion moved to Cyprus to take part in internal security duties on the troubled island, a British possession since 1878. In the post-war period long-standing tensions between the Turkish and Greek populations erupted into violence and Cyprus quickly became a battleground as Greek-Cypriot guerrillas formed themselves into an underground army, *Ethniki Organosis Kypriakou Agonos* (EOKA, or the National Organisation of Greek Fighters) under the command of Colonel Georgios Grivas. Not to be outdone, the Orthodox Church led by Archbishop Makarios gave substantial moral and political impetus to EOKA and the unrest spilled over into violence and civil disobedience. Between 1955 and 1959 the EOKA 'emergency' claimed the lives of 105 British service personnel, 50 policemen and 240 civilians. During the tour of duty the main part of the battalion was based at Limni Camp, with C and D Companies at Polemi Camp, both of which consisted largely of tented accommodation, with huts for messes and cookhouses. The absence of metalled roads turned both into mud baths during wet weather. The main duties were cordon and search operations to hamper the terrorists' movements and to kill any who attempted to breach the cordon. During these operations large numbers of suspects were rounded up and there were several shooting incidents, which thankfully did not create any Argyll casualties.

Eventually an agreement brokered in Zurich at the end of 1958 resolved the situation by paving the way for Cyprus's independence the following year, with a Greek–Cypriot president and a Turkish–Cypriot vice-president. The lowering of tensions allowed the garrison to be reduced and in October 1959 the battalion left the island for a second deployment in West Germany, this time with BAOR at Lemgo near Detmold as part of 20 Armoured Brigade, the other regiments being 9th Lancers and 5th Royal Inniskilling Dragoon Guards. During the tour the battalion was trained to operate Saracen armoured personnel carriers, whose crews came from A Squadron 14/20 Hussars. This was followed by a short tour as public duties battalion in Edinburgh.

At the beginning of 1964 the battalion was on the move again, this time to the Far East, where there was a stand-off between Borneo and Brunei. Trouble had broken out two years earlier over the future of Britain's three remaining colonies in the area – Sarawak, Brunei and Sabah, all of which constituted British Borneo. The prime minister of Malaysia (as Malaya had become in 1963), Tunku Abdul Rahman, wanted to include them in a new Malaysian Federation, but this was opposed by President Ahmed Sukarno of Indonesia who wanted to incorporate the colonies into a greater Indonesia. The first disturbances flared up in Brunei at the end of 1962 but although the rebellion against the sultan was crushed with British support, Sukarno opened a new offensive which became known as the 'Borneo confrontation'. There was a rapid escalation in the violence along the 970-mile land frontier and by the time the Argylls arrived the British contingent in the region had grown to 13 infantry battalions, one battalion of Special Air Service regiment, two regiments each of artillery and engineers, 40 strike aircraft and 80 helicopters, as well as local police and border security force units. Throughout the operation the tactics were similar to those which had been used in Malaya in the previous decade, but in this case greater use was made of helicopters to dominate the jungle.

Before moving into the operational area the battalion was based at Selarang Barracks in Singapore, which provided an opportunity to engage in jungle warfare training in Malacca State as well as to commemorate a memorial plaque to 2nd Argyll and Sutherland Highlanders in the Presbyterian Church. While serving in Singapore the battalion carried out three tours of duty in Borneo, the first of which began in April 1964 in the Belait and Tutong districts. The tasks facing the Argylls included protection of the Shell installations at Seria, prevention of infiltration by Indonesian-backed guerrillas and the provision of support for the local police and security forces. Sukarno's tactics were relatively simple: to promote limited operations along the borders of Sarawak, Brunei and Sabah which could cause enough trouble to delay the formation of the Malaysian Federation and to make life difficult for the opposing security forces. At the time the Director of Operations was Major-General Walter Walker, a forceful Gurkha officer who brooked no nonsense and was a great believer in offensive operations, using SAS patrols, flying in artillery by helicopter to provide fire support and, above all, taking the war to the Indonesians. Under his direction 'Claret' operations were instigated to allow units to mount raids into Indonesian territory, planned and executed to inflict decisive but limited damage to the enemy's forward bases. Kept top secret at the time, their existence only became known a decade later. Every operation had to be sanctioned by Walker, who issued eight 'Golden Rules', the last of which read: 'On no account must any soldier taking part be captured by the enemy – alive or dead.'

In the first instance Claret operations were carried out by the SAS and Gurkha battalions, but in time they were entrusted to British infantry battalions including the Argylls. In the BBC radio documentary series *The Savage Wars of Peace*, Alec Grant, a signaller in the Argylls, recalled the tensions of an ambush and the subsequent pursuit back to the border:

> I remember sitting at the rear of the ambush, being the signaller, with the tracker dog – a very nice Labrador – and his handler, and it was amazing to see the reaction of his dog. You could tell immediately when they were coming because the dog stood up and pointed – and that gave us at least two or three minutes' warning before they actually arrived and the ambush itself. That was quite comforting because we were terrified at the time, but that was my one and only contact message that I sent in Borneo. Trying to get through on voice was just impossible so I switched to morse code and I remember sending 'Contact, contact, contact'.

Following the ambush the site was cleared of dead bodies, which were hung from the trees to prevent them being eaten by wild pigs. All told, the Argylls carried out three six-month tours of duty and the experience added immeasurably to the battalion's capacity to mount low intensity operations – junior leaders often took on the responsibilities of officers, and subalterns frequently found themselves looking after areas of responsibility which would normally have been given to battalion commanders. In November 1966 the battalion returned to Britain, its new base being Seaton Barracks in Plymouth, but it was not long before it was on the move again under the command of Lieutenant-Colonel Colin Mitchell, who had served in the Argylls during the Second World War with the 8th battalion and in Korea, Cyprus and Borneo with the 1st battalion.

The new destination was Aden, where British rule was in its final throes following a presence which stretched back over 128 years. During the steam age the port had been a vital coaling station on the sea route to India through the Suez Canal, and following the Suez debacle it became a major military base and the headquarters of Middle East Command. There had already been outbreaks of trouble in the Radfan hinterland earlier in the decade and by the time the Argylls arrived in June 1967 there was a state of virtual civil war between the two opposing factions – the National Liberation Front (NLF) and the Front for the Liberation of South Yemen (FLOSY). Before the deployment the battalion was put through a rigorous training regime organised by Mitchell. Acclimatisation was assisted by training in the garrison gym with the heat turned up and the Crownhill area of the barracks was turned into a replica of the Crater district of Aden, in which the battalion would be operating. Mitchell even used soldiers dressed as journalists and UN observers to add to the realism. At the beginning of June he led an enlarged advance party to Aden so that senior commanders could spend time gaining useful information from their counterparts in 1st Royal Northumberland Fusiliers, whom the Argylls were replacing.

Although the strict training regime paid dividends during the Argylls' tour of duty, there was tragedy on 20 June when two Land Rovers carrying a joint Fusiliers/Argyll patrol were ambushed in Crater by mutineers from the Aden Armed Police. Amongst the dead were Major Bryan Malcolm and Privates 'Pocus' Hunter and Johnny Moores of the Argylls' recce platoon. Attempts to retrieve the bodies came to nothing because Headquarters Middle East Land Forces refused permission for the armoured cars of Queen's Dragoon Guards to fire their 76mm heavy weapons, and feelings were running high. By this time the rest of the battalion had arrived and on 25 June Mitchell assumed responsibility for the Crater area. Although the general military opinion was that any attempt to re-occupy Crater would end in bloodshed, Mitchell pressed ahead with plans to mount such an operation and these were accepted by his superior officers. Aware that the crisis had received wide press coverage in the British media, Mitchell also made sure that those journalists in Aden were kept in touch with his plans.

The resulting operation was a resounding success and a few days later the Argylls were front-page news. Although many within the army dismissed the battalion's feat as a straightforward walk-in, its very simplicity and audacity made the occupation a resounding triumph which was carried out under the eyes of the accompanying journalists. The advance began at 19.00 on 3 July when B Company, under the command of Major Patrick Palmer and supported by the armoured cars of A Squadron Queen's Dragoon Guards, advanced along Marine Drive and headed towards Crater. As they did so, Pipe Major Robson sounded the charge 'Monymusk' and an hour later the first objectives, the Legislative Council building and the Chartered Bank building, had been seized. Having done that, Mitchell requested permission to exploit the situation by taking the rest of Crater and this was given by the brigade major, Brigadier Charles Dunbar. As Mitchell recalled in his memoirs, 'This was the rewarding moment for any commander, when you know your own chaps will cut through the opposition like a knife through butter. You can feel it in the air and breathe in the aggressive confidence. We were in luck.'

After the humiliations caused by the earlier killing of the British soldiers the Argylls' feat in retaking Crater was a huge boost to morale and Mitchell, now christened 'Mad Mitch' by the press, was the hero of the hour. But there was more to the operation than grabbing headlines. With Crater back under control the battalion set about the task of restoring law and order. The battalion headquarters was set up in the Chartered Bank building and renamed 'Stirling Castle' and Crater was divided into three administrative areas controlled by the three rifle companies. The pipes and drums were also much in evidence. A sense of realism was imposed when Mitchell stated his determination that there should be no repetition of the police murders. 'If you have no ammunition you are to go in with the bayonet,' he told his men. 'It's better that the whole battalion dies in Crater to rescue one Jock than that any one of us comes out alive.' Known as 'Argyll Law', Mitchell's no-nonsense approach restored the peace, but the battalion's robust methods attracted criticism from the general officer commanding Aden, Major-General Philip Tower, who ordered Mitchell to 'throttle back'. As a result there were further outbreaks of violence – Lance-Corporal Willie Orr was shot dead on 21 July – and later there would be allegations, all unfounded, that the men of the Argylls had indulged in brutality towards the local population.

The deployment lasted until the end of November, when the government finally decided to abandon Aden. In conditions of great secrecy 1st Argyll and Sutherland Highlanders withdrew from Crater on the night of 25/26 November and, together with 1st Parachute Regiment and 45 Royal Marine Commando, made its way to the carrier HMS *Albion*. During that strenuous tour of duty the battalion lost five soldiers killed and 24 wounded. Just over six months later came the bombshell news that under stringent defence cuts the army was to be reduced from 200,000 to 165,000 soldiers by 1971 and that 17 major fighting units were to be disbanded – four armoured regiments, four artillery regiments, one engineer regiment and eight infantry regiments. Amongst the latter were The Cameronians (the junior Lowland regiment) and The Argyll and Sutherland Highlanders (the junior Highland regiment). Almost immediately a 'Save the Argylls' campaign was launched, a petition raised over a million signatures and the clever use of the regiment's diced bonnet became an iconic symbol. All this mattered to the people of Scotland and such was the enthusiasm generated that public opinion won the day. In August 1970, following a change of government, the new Conservative administration announced that the regiment would not be disbanded but would be reduced to company strength with 126 officers and soldiers. On 20 January 1971 there came into being 1st Battalion The Argyll and Sutherland Highlanders (Princess Louise's) Balaklava Company under the command of Major Ian Purves Home. Its first deployment as an independent unit was to Gibraltar (May–November) but already it was clear that full restoration was in the offing due to an outbreak of violence in Northern Ireland in 1969 and the need for British troops to assist the civil power in restoring order following outbreaks of sectarian violence in Belfast and Londonderry.

Between then and 31 July 2007, when Operation Banner finally came to an end, Northern Ireland was almost a second home for the regiment. In response to the need the full battalion was re-formed at Ritchie Camp, Kirknewton, under the command of Lieutenant-Colonel Patrick Palmer. Its first tour began in July 1972, shortly after the Stormont parliament had been abolished and direct rule from London introduced. The main opponents were the Provisional Irish Republican Army, but trouble was also fomented by unionist terrorist groups and other troublemakers. Operating in the trying conditions of South Down and Armagh – a nationalist stronghold – the battalion lost two officers and seven soldiers killed and several more wounded. Each subsequent tour brought its own challenges in helping to keep the peace and maintain a sense of proportion in one of the most difficult and longest-lasting counter-insurgency wars fought by the British Army.

The emergency tours of duty in Northern Ireland and deployments with BAOR were very much part of the battalion's way of life in the last two decades of the twentieth century. In November 1979 there was a change of pace when the battalion moved to Hong Kong to assist the authorities in preventing illegal immigrants crossing the border from China. April 1982 saw the battalion in Cyprus before deployments in Edinburgh (1984–86) and Colchester (1986–88). During this latter period the battalion also had a tour of duty in the Falklands, which had almost been lost to an Argentine invasion four years earlier. At the end of the decade the Argylls retrained as a mechanised infantry battalion with 11 Armoured Brigade as part of BAOR in Minden. In 1992 the Options for Change defence cuts proposed that the army should be reduced from 155,000 to 116,000 soldiers and that the infantry should lose 17 of their 55 battalions as a result of the end of the Cold War following the disintegration of the Soviet Union and the reunification of the two Germanys. Although the regiment was spared, the reprieve was to be shortlived. Twelve years later, as a result of the Strategic Defence Review of July 2004, it was decided that the size of the infantry would be reduced still further. While these changes were being discussed the battalion was serving in Iraq as part of the peacekeeping forces deployed in the country in the wake of the previous year's US-led operations to depose President Saddam Hussein.

This time the change was even more radical and far-reaching

as it involved a comprehensive restructuring of the infantry. Under these changes the size of the infantry was reduced from 40 to 36 battalions, and that meant the end of the remaining 19 single-battalion regiments. In their place 15 regiments came into being – five foot guards, nine new large regiments with several operational battalions and one Irish regiment. In Scotland the new formation was called The Royal Regiment of Scotland, and The Argyll and Sutherland Highlanders formed its 5th battalion. At the time of the amalgamation, on 28 March 2006, the 5th battalion was serving in Canterbury, Kent where it formed part of 16 Air Assault Brigade. Naturally the changes were the subject of a good deal of sadness but the colonel of the new regiment, Major-General Andrew Graham, a distinguished Argyll, insisted that the 'golden thread' with past history and traditions would continue to be maintained. The fighting traditions of the constituent parts also remained unsullied. In the spring of 2008, 111 years after the 2nd Argyll and Sutherland Highlanders served in the Tochi Valley, The Argyll and Sutherland Highlanders, 5th battalion, The Royal Regiment of Scotland deployed to Helmand province in southern Afghanistan with 16 Air Assault Brigade as part of the NATO-led International Security Assistance Forces.

Appendix

REGIMENTAL FAMILY TREE

1st battalion (91st)

1794: 98th (Argyllshire Highlanders) Foot

1798: 91st (Argyllshire Highlanders) Foot

1804: 2nd battalion raised

1809: 91st Regiment of Foot

1815: 2nd battalion disbanded

1864: 91st (Argyllshire Highlanders)

1872: 91st Princess Louise's Argyllshire Highlanders

1881: 1st Princess Louise's Sutherland and Argyll Highlanders

1882: 1st Princess Louise's (Argyll and Sutherland Highlanders)

1920: 1st The Argyll and Sutherland Highlanders (Princess Louise's)

1947: 1st and 2nd battalions amalgamated

2nd battalion (93rd)

1799: 93rd (Highland) Regiment of Foot

1813: 2nd battalion raised

1815: 2nd battalion disbanded

1861: 93rd Sutherland Highlanders
1881: 2nd Princess Louise's Sutherland and Argyll Highlanders
1882: 2nd Princess Louise's (Argyll and Sutherland Highlanders)
1920: 2nd The Argyll and Sutherland Highlanders (Princess Louise's)
1947: 1st and 2nd battalions amalgamated

91st/93rd

1947: 1st battalion The Argyll and Sutherland Highlanders
(Princess Louise's)
1970: reduced to 1st battalion The Argyll and Sutherland
Highlanders Balaklava Company (Princess Louise's)
1972: 1st battalion The Argyll and Sutherland Highlanders
(Princess Louise's) reformed
2006: The Argyll and Sutherland Highlanders, 5th battalion, The
Royal Regiment of Scotland

REGIMENTAL BADGE

The regimental badge is a circle inscribed 'Argyll and Sutherland' surrounded by a wreath of thistles. In the centre, the cypher of Princess Louise reversed and interlaced with the princess's coronet mounted above. The boar's head of the Duke of Argyll and the cat of the Duke of Sutherland lie within the circle. The regiment has two mottos: *Ne Obliviscaris* (Do not forget), the motto of the Duke of Argyll and *Sans Peur* (Without fear), the motto of the Duke of Sutherland.

REGIMENTAL TARTANS

Both the 91st and the 93rd originally wore the Government or Black Watch tartan. Between 1809 and 1864 the 91st lost its Highland status and the right to wear the kilt. On being restored to Highland status the 91st wore trews in Campbell of Cawdor tartan until 1881. On amalgamation the 91st and 93rd reverted to Government tartan, but of a slightly lighter shade. Officers and senior non-commissioned officers wore green silk panelling on the front flap of the kilt.

REGIMENTAL PIPE MUSIC

Pipers were not officially recognised by the army until 1854, when all Highland regiments were allowed a Pipe-Major and five pipers. Before that most Highland regiments employed pipers as a regimental expense and these were distributed throughout the regiment disguised on the muster roll as 'drummers'. The pipes and drums were always fully trained infantry soldiers and were in addition to the military band, which existed until 1994.

The regiment's pipe music is regularised as follows:
March Past in Quick Time: Highland Laddie, The Campbells are Coming
The Charge: Monymusk
Company Marches: At discretion of the commanding officer
Funerals: Lochaber

BATTLE HONOURS

Two colours are carried by the regiment, the King's or Queen's, which is the Union flag, and the Regimental Colour (originally First and Second Colour) which is buff.

During the Napoleonic wars battle honours were added to the colours. In their final form, those gained during the First World War and the Second World War are carried on the Queen's Colour and the remainder are carried on the Regimental Colour. At the outset battle honours were given sparingly or even randomly: in 1882 the system of battle honours was revised by a War Office committee under the chairmanship of General Sir Archibald Alison. It laid down guidelines whereby only victories would be included and the majority of the regiment had to be present. Additional refinements were made in 1907 and 1909 and their recommendations form the basis of the regiment's pre-1914 battle honours.

Pre-1914 (91st and 93rd)

Cape of Good Hope 1806	**Orthes**	**Lucknow**
Rolica	**Toulouse**	**South Africa 1879**
Vimiera	**Peninsula**	
Corunna	**South Africa 1846–47, 1851, '52, '53**	**Modder River**
Pyrenees	**Alma**	**Paardeberg**
Nivelle	**Balaklava**	**South Africa 1899–1902**
Nive	**Sevastopol**	

After the First World War there were further refinements to take cognisance of the size and complexity of the conflict. It was agreed that each regiment could carry ten major honours on their King's Colour, but supporting operations would also receive battle honours which would not be displayed. The battle honours in bold type are carried on the Queen's Colour.

The First World War (27 battalions)

Mons	Ancre Heights	Amiens
Le Cateau	Ancre 1916	Hindenburg Line
Retreat from Mons	**Arras, 1917, '18**	Epehy
Marne, 1914, '18	Scarpe 1917, '18	Canal du Nord
Aisne 1914	Arleux	St Quentin Canal
La Bassée 1914	Pilckem	Beaurevoir

APPENDIX

Messines 1914, '18

Armentières 1914

Ypres 1915, '17, '18

Gravenstafel

St Julien

Frezenberg

Bellewaarde

Festubert 1915

Loos

Somme 1916, '18

Albert 1916, '18

Bazentin

Delville Wood

Pozieres

Flers–Courcelette

Morval

Le Transloy

Menin Road

Polygon Wood

Broodseinde

Poelcapelle

Passchendaele

Cambrai 1917, '18

St Quentin

Bapaume 1918

Rosieres

Lys

Estaires

Hazebrouck

Bailleul

Kemmel

Bethune

Soissonais–Ourcq

Tardenois

Courtrai

Selle

Sambre

France and
Flanders
1914–18

Italy 1917–18

Struma

**Doiran
1917, '18**

Macedonia
1915–18

Gallipoli
1915–18

Rumani

Egypt 1916

Gaza

El Mughar

Nebi Samwil

Jaffa

Palestine
1917–18

In 1956 it was agreed to treat the Second World War in the same way as the previous conflict. Those in bold type appear on the Queen's Colour.

The Second World War (seven battalions)

Somme 1940

Odon

Tourmauville Bridge

Caen

NW Europe
1940, 44–45

Abyssinia 1941

Sidi Barrani

Cassino II

Liri Valley

Aquino

Monte Casalino

Esquay

Mont Pincon

Quarry Hill

Estry

Falaise

Dives Crossing

Aart

Lower Maas

Meijil

Venlo Pocket

Ourthe

Rhineland

Reichswald

Rhine

Uelzen

Artlenberg

El Alamein

Medenine

Akarit

Djebel Azzag 1942

Kef Quiba Pass

Mine de Sedjenane

Medjez Plain

Longstop Hill 1943

North Africa 1940–43

Landing in Sicily

Gerbini

Adrano

Centuripe

Sicily 1943

Termoli

Sangro

Monte Spaduro

Monte Grande

Senio

Santerno
  Crossing

Argenta Gap

Italy 1943–45

Crete

Heraklion

Middle East
  1941

North Malaya

Grik Road

Central Malaya

Ipoh

Slim River

Singapore
  Island

**Malaya
  1941–42**

Post 1945 (1ˢᵗ battalion)

Pakchon   **Korea 1950–51**

ALLIED AND AFFILIATED REGIMENTS
Canada

The Argyll and Sutherland Highlanders of Canada
  (Princess Louise's)
The Calgary Highlanders

Australia

The Royal New South Wales Regiment

Pakistan

1ˢᵗ battalion (Scinde) The Frontier Force Regiment

WINNERS OF THE VICTORIA CROSS

Captain W.G.D. Stewart, 93ʳᵈ Sutherland Highlanders, Indian Mutiny, 1857

A veteran of the Crimean War, William George Drummond Stewart was awarded the Victoria Cross for courageously and successfully leading a charge to capture two enemy guns at the Sikandarbagh during the second relief of Lucknow on 16 November 1857 (one of six VCs awarded to the 93ʳᵈ that day). A native of Grandtully in Perthshire, he died in 1868 aged 37 whilst demonstrating a sword-swallowing trick.

Colour-Sergeant James Munro, 93ʳᵈ Sutherland Highlanders, Indian Mutiny, 1857

During the same action at the Sikandarbagh James Munro rescued an officer who was in danger of being cut down by mutineers. Born at Nigg in Easter Ross, Munro died on 15 February 1871 and is buried in Craigdunan Cemetery in Inverness.

Sergeant John Paton, 93ʳᵈ Sutherland Highlanders, Indian Mutiny, 1857

Once the Sikandarbagh had been captured the Shah Najaf mosque was attacked. Following a heavy artillery bombardment Sergeant Paton led his men into the building and completed its capture. After leaving the army he emigrated to Australia, where he died in April 1914.

Lance-Corporal John Dunlay, 93rd Sutherland Highlanders, Indian Mutiny, 1857

One of the many Irish soldiers to have served in a Scottish regiment, Dunlay took part in the fighting to capture the Sikandarbagh, where he entered the breaches to save an officer. During the action he was shot in the knee and the offending bullet can still be seen attached to his medal in the Sheesh Mahal Museum in Patiala.

Private Peter Grant, 93rd Sutherland Highlanders, Indian Mutiny, 1857

Another Irishman, Peter Grant was awarded the Victoria Cross for his gallantry in defending a senior officer who had grabbed the mutineers' colours. During the action he killed five rebel sepoys with his sword. He was drowned in the River Tay on 10 January 1868 and is buried in the Eastern Necropolis in Dundee.

Private David Mackay, 93rd Sutherland Highlanders, Indian Mutiny, 1857

The sixth VC to be awarded to the 93rd was won by David Mackay for his courage in capturing a mutineers' standard and fighting off the attempts to retake it. A native of Caithness, he died in Lesmahagow, Lanarkshire, in 1880.

Lieutenant William McBean, 93rd Sutherland Highlanders, Indian Mutiny, 1857

Commissioned from the ranks and aged 40, McBean demonstrated astonishing bravery and fortitude in killing 11 mutineers at the Begum Bagh using only a rusty knife and his bare hands. His final victim was despatched at sword-point. When he was presented with his medal and congratulated for a good day's work he said: 'Tutts, it didna' tak' me 20 minutes!' He retired in the rank of major-general and died in London in June 1878.

Captain J.A. Liddell, 3ʳᵈ Argyll and Sutherland Highlanders and Royal Flying Corps, First World War, 1915

A native of Newcastle-on-Tyne, John Aidan Liddell was commissioned in The Argyll and Sutherland Highlanders but won his Victoria Cross while serving in the Royal Flying Corps. Whilst flying his RE5 aircraft over enemy lines on 31 July 1915 he was attacked and badly wounded in the right thigh. This caused him to black out but he recovered and managed to land behind Allied lines. He died a month later aged 27.

Lieutenant J.R.N. Graham, 9ᵗʰ Argyll and Sutherland Highlanders, First World War, 1917

While commanding 136ᵗʰ Coy, Machine-Gun Corps in Mesopotamia, John Reginald Noble Graham came under heavy enemy fire which caused heavy casualties amongst his men. Despite the risks, Graham exposed himself to the enemy fire to fetch ammunition and reopened fire on the enemy. Although wounded, he continued until he was forced to retire. He retired from the army in the rank of lieutenant-colonel and died in Edinburgh on 6 December 1980 aged 88.

Captain Arthur Henderson, 4ᵗʰ Argyll and Sutherland Highlanders, First World War, 1917

During an attack on the German lines at Fontaine-les-Croiselles Captain Henderson was badly wounded but, undeterred, he led his men to their objective. He then held the position and his coolness and good humour under fire offered huge encouragement to his men. Later in the action he was killed by enemy fire and is buried at Cojeul British Cemetery at St Martin-le-Cojeul.

2nd Lieutenant J.C. Buchan, 7th Argyll and Sutherland Highlanders, First World War, 1918

During an enemy attack near Marteville on 21 March 1918 John Crawford Buchan, a native of Alloa, was badly wounded but refused to retire. Despite being under constant bombardment he continued to visit his posts to encourage his men and refused all offers to surrender. Eventually he was cut off and was last seen fighting against overwhelming odds. He is buried in Roisel Communal Cemetery Extension.

Lieutenant D.L. MacIntyre, Argyll and Sutherland Highlanders, First World War, 1918

David Lowe MacIntyre was awarded the Victoria Cross while attached to 1/6th Highland Light Infantry during an attack on the British lines near Henin and Fontaine which began on 24 August 1918. While acting as adjutant he was constantly in the line offering encouragement to the men. Later he led a party to put a machine-gun post out of action and rushed another post single-handed. He died in Edinburgh in 1967 aged 72.

Lieutenant W.D. Bissett, 1/6th Argyll and Sutherland Highlanders, First World War, 1918

During an enemy attack near Maing William Davidson Bissett took over command of his company and managed to withdraw them to a nearby railway line. Although his left flank had been turned Bissett showed great resourcefulness by calling on his men to make a bayonet charge which drove back the enemy. He died at Wrexham in May 1971.

APPENDIX

Lieutenant-Colonel L.M. Campbell, 7th Argyll and Sutherland Highlanders, Second World War, 1943

On 6 April 1943 at Wadi Akarit, Tunisia, the battalion commanded by Lorne MacLaine Campbell had to break through an enemy minefield and anti-tank ditch in order to form a bridgehead. The battalion formed up in darkness and then attacked at an angle. This difficult operation was successfully completed and at least 600 prisoners were taken. Next day the position was subjected to heavy and continuous bombardment but under Campbell's inspiring leadership the bridgehead was held. He died at the family home, The Airds in Argyllshire, on 25 May 1981.

Major J.T. McK. Anderson, 8th Argyll and Sutherland Highlanders, Second World War, 1943

On 23 April 1943 at Longstop Hill, Tunisia, John Thompson McKellar ('Jack') Anderson assumed command of the battalion when his commanding officer was killed. Later he was wounded in the leg but went on and eventually achieved the military objective. Although his battalion was reduced to about 44 officers and men, 200 prisoners were taken and he personally led successful attacks on several machine-gun posts and mortar emplacements. Anderson was killed in Italy six months later.

Major Kenneth Muir, 1st Argyll and Sutherland Highlanders, Korean War, 1950

During an attack on Hill 282 on 23 September 1950, B and C Companies came under heavy enemy mortar- and shell-fire. As the situation deteriorated the commanding officer called for a US air strike and although recognition panels were displayed the pilots mistakenly attacked the Argyll position. This forced the men to withdraw to a lower position before Muir organised a counter-attack. While lending encouragement to his men Muir was mortally wounded. His last words spoke only of defiance: 'The Gooks [North Koreans] will never drive the Argylls off this hill.' All the wounded men were eventually evacuated.

Bibliography

Unless otherwise stated extracts from soldiers' letters and diaries are in the possession of the regiment or are housed in the Imperial War Museum or the National Army Museum, London. Quotations from battalion and brigade War Diaries or other official papers are housed in the National Archives, Kew. Use has also been made of recordings from two BBC Radio programmes featuring the regiment: *The Savage Wars of Peace,* by Charles Allan, Radio 4, 1988–1989 and *Seven Hundred Glengarried Men*, by Trevor Royle, BBC Radio Scotland, July 1997.

BOOKS ABOUT THE ARGYLL AND SUTHERLAND HIGHLANDERS

Anderson, Brigadier R.C.B., *History of the Argyll and Sutherland Highlanders, 1ˢᵗ Battalion 1908–1939*, Constable, Edinburgh, 1954; *History of the Argyll and Sutherland Highlanders, 1ˢᵗ Battalion 1939–1954*, Constable, Edinburgh, 1956

Barker, Lieutenant-Colonel F.R.P., *History of the Argyll and Sutherland Highlanders, 9ᵗʰ Battalion, 54 Light AA Regiment*,

1939–1945, Thomas Nelson, London, 1950

Barr, James Craig, *Home Service: The Recollections of a Commanding Officer serving in Great Britain during the War, 1914–1919*, privately published, 1920

Burgoyne, Richard, *Historical Records of the 93rd Highlanders*, Richard Bentley, London, 1883

Cameron, Captain I.C., *History of the Argyll and Sutherland Highlanders, 7th Battalion from El Alamein to Germany*, Thomas Nelson, London, 1946

Campbell, Alastair, of Airds, *Argyll & Sutherland Highlanders*, Tempus, Stroud, 2005

Cavendish, Brigadier A.E.J., *Am Reisimeid Chataich: The 93rd Sutherland Highlanders*, privately published, 1928

Dunn-Pattison, R.P., *The History of the 91st Argyllshire Highlanders*, William Blackwood, Edinburgh and London, 1910

Flower, Desmond, *History of the Argyll and Sutherland Highlanders, 5th Battalion, 1939–1945*, Thomas Nelson, London, 1950

Goff, G.L., *Historical Records of the 91st Argyllshire Highlanders*, Richard Bentley, London, 1881

Graham, Lieutenant-Colonel F.C.C., *History of the Argyll and Sutherland Highlanders, 1st Battalion, 1939–1945*, Thomas Nelson, London, 1949

Groves, Lieutenant-Colonel Percy, *History of the 91st Princess Louise's Argyllshire Highlanders*, W. & E.K. Johnston, Edinburgh, 1894; *History of the 93rd Sutherland Highlanders*, W. & E.K. Johnston, Edinburgh, 1894

Hay, Ian (real name John Hay Beith), *The First Hundred Thousand*, William Blackwood, Edinburgh and London, 1915

Malcolm, Lieutenant-Colonel A.D., *History of the Argyll and Sutherland Highlanders, 8th Battalion, 1939–1945*, Thomas Nelson, London, 1949

BIBLIOGRAPHY

Malcolm, Lieutenant-Colonel G.I., of Poltalloch, *The Argylls in Korea*, Thomas Nelson, London, 1952; *The Argyllshire Highlanders, 1860–1960*, Holbeid Press, Glasgow, 1960

McElwee, Major W.L., *History of the Argyll and Sutherland Highlanders, 2nd Battalion 1944–1945*, Thomas Nelson, London, 1949

Mileham, P.J.R., *Fighting Highlanders: The History of the Argyll and Sutherland Highlanders*, Arms and Armour Press, London, 1993

Mitchell, Lieutenant-Colonel Colin, *Having Been A Soldier*, Hamish Hamilton, London, 1969

Munro, Surgeon-General William, *Reminiscences of Military Service with the 93rd Highlanders*, Hurst and Blackett, London, 1883; *Records of Service and Campaigning in Many Lands*, 2 vols, Hurst and Blackett, London, 1877

Pratt, Paul, ed., *History of the Argyll and Sutherland Highlanders, 6th Battalion, 93rd Anti-Tank Regiment RA (A & SH)*, Thomas Nelson, London, 1949

Rose, Angus, *Who Dies Fighting*, London, Cape, 1944

Sotheby, Lieutenant-Colonel H.G., *The 10th Battalion, Argyll and Sutherland Highlanders, 1914–1919*, John Murray, London, 1931

Stewart, Major-General Sir David, of Garth, *Sketches of the Character, Manners and Present State of the Highlanders of Scotland, with Details of the Military Service of the Highland Regiments*, 2 vols, Constable, Edinburgh, 1822

Stewart, Brigadier I. MacA., *History of the Argyll and Sutherland Highlanders, 2nd Battalion (The Thin Red Line), Malaya Campaign, 1941–1942*, Thomas Nelson, London, 1947

Sutherland, Douglas, *The Argyll and Sutherland Highlanders*, Leo Cooper, London, 1969

OTHER BOOKS CONSULTED

Ascoli, David, *A Companion to the British Army 1660–1983*, Harrap, London, 1983

Barnett, Correlli, *Britain and her Army 1509–1970*, Allen Lane, London, 1970; *The Lost Victory: British Dreams, British Realities 1945–1950*, Macmillan, London, 1995

Baynes, John, with Laffin, John, *Soldiers of Scotland*, Brassey's, London, 1988

Bewsher, Major F.W., *The History of the 51st (Highland) Division 1914–1918*, William Blackwood, Edinburgh and London, 1921

Brereton, J.M., *The British Army: A Social History of the British Army from 1661 to the Present Day*, The Bodley Head, London, 1986

Chandler, David, and Beckett, Ian, eds, *The Oxford Illustrated History of the British Army*, Oxford University Press, Oxford, 1994

Churchill, Winston S., *Frontiers and Wars*, Eyre & Spottiswood, London, 1962

David, Saul, *Churchill's Sacrifice of the Highland Division*, Brassey's, London, 1994; *The Indian Mutiny 1857*, Viking, London, 2002

Delaforce, Patrick, *Monty's Highlanders: 51st Highland Division in World War Two*, Tom Donovan, Brighton, 1997

Doyle, Arthur Conan, *The Great Boer War*, Smith Elder, London, 1900

Ewing, John, *History of the 9th (Scottish) Division 1914–1919*, John Murray, London, 1921

Forbes-Mitchell, William, *Reminiscences of the Great Mutiny*, Macmillan, London, 1893

Fortescue, Sir John, *A History of the British Army*, 13 vols, Macmillan, London, 1899–1930

Henderson, Diana M., *Highland Soldier 1820–1920*, John Donald, Edinburgh, 1989; *The Scottish Regiments*, Collins, Glasgow, 1996

BIBLIOGRAPHY

Holmes, Richard, ed., *The Oxford Companion to Military History*, Oxford University Press, Oxford, 2001

Jackson, Bill and Bramall, Dwin, *The Chiefs: The Story of the United Kingdom Chiefs of Staff*, Brassey's, London, 1992

Keegan, John, *Six Armies in Normandy*, Jonathan Cape, London, 1982

Kinglake, A.W., *The Invasion of the Crimea*, 8 vols, William Blackwood, Edinburgh and London, 1863–87

Linklater, Eric, *Our Men in Korea*, HMSO, London, 1954

Martin, Lieutenant-General H.G., *The Fifteenth Scottish Division 1939–1945*, William Blackwood, Edinburgh and London, 1948

Massey, W.T., *How Jerusalem was Won, Being the Record of Allenby's Campaign in Palestine*, Constable, London, 1919

Masters, John, *Bugles and a Tiger*, Michael Joseph, London, 1956

Mileham, P.J.R., *Scottish Regiments*, Spellmount, Tunbridge Wells, 1988

Neillands, Robin, *A Fighting Retreat: The British Empire 1947–1997*, Hodder & Stoughton, London, 1996

Roberts, Lord, *Forty-One Years in India*, 2 vols, Richard Bentley, London, 1897

Royle, Trevor, *The Best Years of Their Lives: The National Service Experience 1945–1963*, Michael Joseph, London, 1986; *Crimea: The Great Crimean War 1854–1856*, Little Brown, London, 1999

Salmond, J.B., *The History of the 51ˢᵗ Highland Division 1939–1945*, William Blackwood, Edinburgh and London, 1953

Shepherd, Naomi, *Ploughing Sand: British Rule in Palestine 1917–1948*, John Murray, London, 1999

Stewart, J, and Buchan, John, *The 15ᵗʰ (Scottish) Division 1914–1919*, William Blackwood, Edinburgh and London, 1926

Strawson, John, *Gentlemen in Khaki: The British Army 1890–1990*, Hutchinson, London, 1989; *Beggars in Red: The British Army 1789–1889*, Hutchinson, London, 1991

Wakefield, Alan, and Moody, Simon, *Under the Devil's Eye: Britain's Forgotten Army at Salonika 1915–1918*, Sutton Publishing, Stroud, 2004

Wood, Stephen, *The Scottish Soldier*, Archive Publications, Manchester, 1987

WEBSITES

Diary of Robert Lindsay Mackay: http://lu.softxs.ch/mackay/RLM_Diary.html

Museum of the Argyll and Sutherland Highlanders: http://www.aboutscotland.com/argylls/contact.html

Index

INDEX

INDEX

INDEX

INDEX

INDEX